I.E.

JAMIE McGHEE
GRIANAN
KILMOROCK
BY BEAULY

Young Readers Nature Library

EARLY MAN

Young Readers Nature Library

Adapted from the LIFE Nature Library

EARLY MAN

F. Clark Howell

and the Editors of TIME-LIFE BOOKS

TIME-LIFE BOOKS, ALEXANDRIA, VIRGINIA

ON THE COVER: This skull of a Neanderthal
man was among 10 skeletons found on
Mount Carmel, in what is now Israel, in
the 1930s. The Neanderthals, who lived
between 100,000 and 40,000 years ago, are
thought to be ancestors of modern man.

Other Publications:
THE SEAFARERS
THE ENCYCLOPEDIA OF COLLECTIBLES
THE GREAT CITIES
WORLD WAR II
HOME REPAIR AND IMPROVEMENT
THE WORLD'S WILD PLACES
THE TIME-LIFE LIBRARY OF BOATING
HUMAN BEHAVIOR
THE ART OF SEWING
THE OLD WEST
THE EMERGENCE OF MAN
THE AMERICAN WILDERNESS
THE TIME-LIFE ENCYCLOPEDIA OF GARDENING
LIFE LIBRARY OF PHOTOGRAPHY
THIS FABULOUS CENTURY
FOODS OF THE WORLD
TIME-LIFE LIBRARY OF AMERICA
TIME-LIFE LIBRARY OF ART
GREAT AGES OF MAN
LIFE SCIENCE LIBRARY
THE LIFE HISTORY OF THE UNITED STATES
TIME READING PROGRAM
LIFE NATURE LIBRARY
LIFE WORLD LIBRARY
FAMILY LIBRARY:
  HOW THINGS WORK IN YOUR HOME
  THE TIME-LIFE BOOK OF THE FAMILY CAR
  THE TIME-LIFE FAMILY LEGAL GUIDE
  THE TIME-LIFE BOOK OF FAMILY FINANCE

Contents

1
Unearthing the First Fossil Clues

Where did man come from? This question has fascinated men for thousands of years. It is responsible for a large number of myths and for many of the world's religions, each attempting to explain the creation of the earth and of men. Many of these explanations are interesting and beautiful, but much of their detail is no longer regarded as strictly factual. Instead, they reflect man's yearning to understand mysteries and his often poetic attempts to construct a good and moral world.

The story of Creation, as told in the Bible, is a fine example. It is seldom taken literally now. Its simple, sweeping concepts are interpreted by most modern Christians and Jews as being symbolic of the spirit and majesty of God. The world was not created in six days, even though the Bible says it was, but this no longer troubles most devout people.

Three hundred years ago most Christians took their Bible literally. Hell was a fiery place beneath their feet. Heaven was "up there" somewhere. Even the age of the earth had been carefully calculated, by Archbishop James Ussher of Armagh, Ire-

AN ANCIENT SKULL, between 40,000 and 60,000 years old, belonged to a type of early man called Neanderthal. The skull looks like ours in some ways, but has thick ridges over the eye sockets and a slanting forehead. By studying such skulls scientists learn much about what man's ancestors were like.

JOHN FRERE
1740-1807

JACQUES BOUCHER DE PERTHES
1788-1868

land, in 1650. His date for Creation was 4004 B.C. and another clergyman came up with the exact day and hour—9 a.m. on October 23.

Who was there to argue with these men? Nobody, really. There was not yet any such thing as modern science and there were no real scientists. The few men who were interested in poking into the ground and in collecting and measuring things were simply curious amateurs. One of these men, a Frenchman named Isaac de la Peyrère, studied a large collection of oddly chipped stones gathered in the French countryside. He was daring enough to publish a book suggesting that these stones had been shaped by primitive men who had lived before the time of Adam. His book was publicly burned in 1655.

But odd-shaped stones continued to turn up. So did even odder-shaped bones. Gradually a few men began to realize that the earth had been inhabited at one time by a great number of creatures that no longer existed—huge mammoths, woolly rhinoceroses, saber-toothed tigers. More digging produced more puzzles. In 1771 human bones were found, together with the remains of extinct cave bears, in a site in Germany—which suggested that there were not only ancient animals but ancient men as well. However, the man who found them did not have the courage to face the logical conclusion, and wrote that the bones must have come together by chance.

Others guessed right but could not get a hearing. In 1790 John Frere found strange stone tools in the same place as the remains of extinct animals at Hoxne in England. Working in Belgian caves in 1830, P. C. Schmerling found many stone objects with

Pioneers in Prehistory

These three investigators were well ahead of their time in their theories of man's ancestors. In 1797 John Frere, a British archeologist, reported finding some axes he believed to be from "a very remote period." Some years later a Frenchman, Jacques Boucher de Perthes, found flint tools next to bones of extinct elephants. He reasoned that the tools and bones were the same age—older than the Great Flood described in the Bible. Another Englishman, Charles Lyell, studied tools found in France. He set their age at 100,000 years, and concluded that if the tools were that old, man must be too.

CHARLES LYELL
1797-1875

the bones of vanished mammoths, and also uncovered two human skulls. These astonishing finds went unnoticed.

It was even difficult to get anyone to realize that stone "tools" were tools at all. The first man to attempt to prove this was a French customs official named Jacques Boucher de Perthes. Interested in archeology, he began poking about in gravel banks near Abbeville in northern France. He was puzzled by the number of flint objects that did not "belong" in the pits because they were made of a different kind of stone and bore unmistakable signs of human workmanship. Many of them were carefully chipped around the edges and looked enough like axes to set anyone thinking. Boucher de Perthes began collecting his finds, and in 1838 and 1839 presented his case for the existence of men far older than any yet known. Two French learned so-

cieties rejected his ideas, and his published findings were ignored for many years.

These early investigators labored under two separate handicaps. First, they lacked a scientific method, and this often made it easier for critics to argue that tools, human bones and extinct animals had come together by accident (or even to claim that the discoverer had "planted" them together).

A second and much more serious handicap was that scientists and laymen alike were suspicious of stone tools and fossils because they still had not the faintest notion of how old the earth actually was. But by the end of the 18th Century a few men were beginning to find some perturbing clues to its long history. They read these clues in the various layers of different kinds of sediments—gravels, sands, marine limestones—that they encountered, one beneath an-

THE MODERN THEORY OF THE DESCENT OF MAN.

other, some of them dozens of feet thick, indicating that they must have been laid down over long periods of time.

From the growing evidence of such layers, an Englishman named Charles Lyell put together a theory called "uniformitarianism." This long word embraces a very simple and logical idea: If the earth's surface is now affected by various forces—wind, flowing water, frost, volcanic activity, mountain building—then it stands to reason that such forces have been operating in a similar, or "uniform," fashion in the past also. After millions of years, these forces left their marks in the varied layers of the earth's crust. The world is constantly remaking itself, and the only reason we are not aware of it is that it happens so slowly. A man who watches a few pebbles fall from a cliff may not realize it, but he is watching the disintegration of a mountain. Muddy water flowing down a river can eventually move billions of tons of material from the center of a continent to the bottom of the sea. This immense layer of mud may harden and be covered in turn by other layers in a process extending over a great span of time. To a society accustomed to believing that the earth was eternal and unchanging and had been created only about 6,000 years ago, this was a staggering revelation.

Lyell's great work on geology was published between 1830 and 1833. Among its readers was a young man named Charles Darwin, who in another 26 years was to publish an even more shattering book, *On the Origin of Species*. Darwin was impressed by the great variety of living organisms, and the obvious relationships of fossils in different layers of the earth. He began to wonder how the different species now in existence might have become so different. He proposed his famous theory of evolution, with natural selection as the principal mechanism that directed change.

Darwin was an extremely cautious man, and the evidence he used to support his theory was limited to plants and some animals; it did not include man. He mentioned the

A Strange Series of Ancestors

In 1867 a naturalist who believed in the new theory of evolution drew these pictures to suggest how man developed from lower animals. He was right in first showing simple animals with few cells *(1-8)*, followed by fish and reptiles *(11-17)*. But few fossils had been discovered where he worked, and he really knew little about evolution. We now know that a duck-billed platypus *(18)* could never have developed into a kangaroo *(19)*, and that such animals were not direct ancestors of modern man.

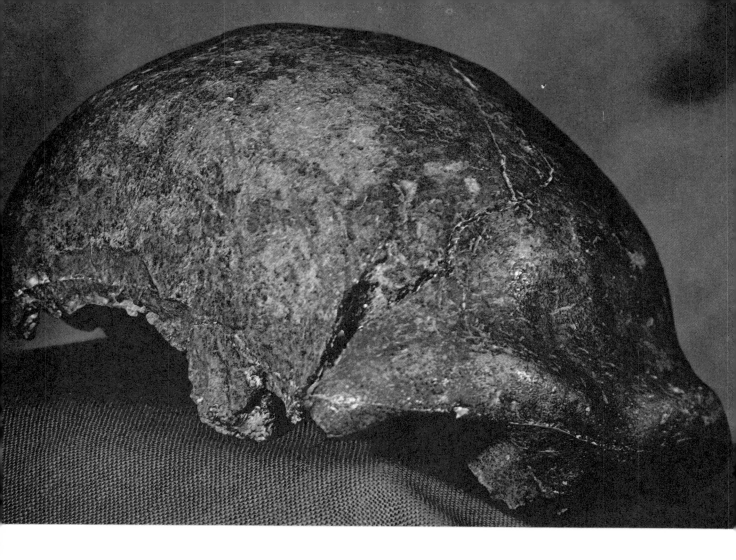

origin of human beings only once in his entire book. And then he permitted himself a single, timid sentence in his conclusion: "Light will be thrown on the origin of man and his history."

But the implication was plain enough, and nobody missed it. Thus at this turning point in the history of knowledge, there emerged two great ideas about the origin of man: that the earth is an extremely ancient planet long populated by many kinds of animals, some of which are no longer living; and that man himself has his origins far back in time. But how far back, and

who those ancestral men were, nobody as yet had even the slightest notion. Everything that we now know about our ancestry we have learned in the last century, and most of it was learned during the last couple of decades.

In 1863 Thomas H. Huxley published a book, *Man's Place in Nature*, that was the first scientific approach to the problem of man's development. By comparing the anatomy of man with that of the apes, Huxley established that the chimpanzee and the gorilla were the two living creatures most closely related to man. He also showed

A Celebrated Hoax

Skulls of ancient man (*at left and directly below*), look
something like crosses between the skull of a modern
man, (*center, below*) and that of an ape. This led to an
amazing hoax in 1912, when an amateur archeologist
dug up what was claimed to be the skull of an early man
(*right*). Forty years later it was proved a fake; it was
actually an ape's jaw skillfully combined with the skull of a
modern man. No one ever found out who buried it, or why.

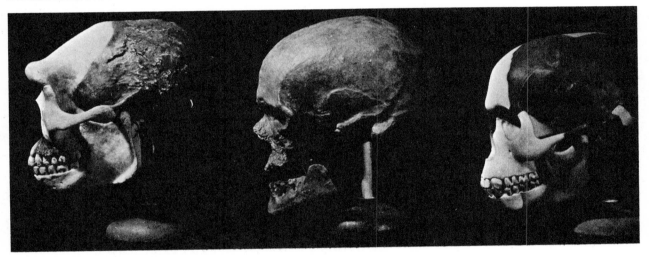

that apes and men had evolved in much
the same way and according to the same
principles. His book was followed in 1871
by Darwin's *The Descent of Man*. Both
were widely misunderstood. Most people—
among them scientists—jumped to the conclusion that both Darwin and Huxley
thought that men were descended directly
from the living apes. In short, a person
who accepted the theory of evolution apparently was obliged to believe that either
a chimpanzee or a gorilla had founded his
family line.

However, man obviously was *not* an ape,

and a distaste for the idea that he might
have been kept many people from accepting
the theory of evolution. It also produced another misconception that was to plague
scientists for years—the idea of a "missing
link." If men were men and apes were
apes, it was argued, the connection could
be proved by discovering a fossil that stood
halfway between the two. But no "missing
link" fossils were found—nor would they
ever be, for we know today that while
both men and apes are descended from common, but very remote ancestors, they bear
the relationship of cousin to cousin rather

than that of grandparent to grandchild.

What the fossil hunters did not realize was that they already had parts of an extinct human in their possession. These were the skullcap and some limb bones dug out of a cave in the limestone cliffs of the Neander valley near Düsseldorf, Germany in 1856. To experts familiar with human skeletons and skull structure, there were some very peculiar things about this "Neanderthal" man, as he came to be known. The skull had strongly developed eyebrow ridges and a retreating forehead. It was also much flatter on top and bulged in the back more than the skull of any modern human being. The renowned German anatomist Rudolf Virchow examined it and declared that its peculiarities were caused by disease and did not indicate primitiveness, as some less famous examiners had suggested.

Thirty years later two skeletons similar to the Neanderthal one were discovered in a cave at Spy, Belgium. This time their great age had to be accepted. The human bones were found in deposits with bones of mammals that no longer exist, as well as with chipped stone implements. All of this material was carefully removed, layer by layer, so that there could be no error about what belonged with what. The evidence was unmistakable. This was another Neanderthal type of man, but not a man identical with the ones who now walk the earth.

Spurred by such discoveries, other sci-

The Fossil-Finding Team

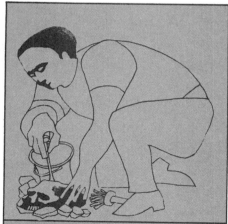

PALEOANTHROPOLOGIST
Digging and studying fossils takes a team of specialists directed by a paleoanthropologist. He chooses the place to dig, supervises the other men and determines the significance of the material found.

GEOLOGIST
Geologists know a great deal about the different layers under the earth, and they can often help in picking the place to dig. They can also help determine the age of fossils that are found in different layers.

SURVEYOR
This specialist makes a map of the entire digging area, showing in detail where it is in relation to natural landmarks. This serves as a working record of the area after it has been torn up by digging.

entists devoted their lives to pushing the record of man's ancestry even farther back in time. One was Eugène Dubois, a young doctor who in the 1880s began to search in the Dutch East Indies. He chose the area because he knew that apes lived there; he reasoned that man's ancestors as they gradually lost their coats of hair must have continued to live in warm regions, and he might find their fossils there. Find them he did. He discovered the famous Java man, who now bears the scientific name of *Homo erectus*. This was a creature so primitive that Dubois himself thought at first that he had only found the scattered remains— a skullcap, lower jaw fragment and several thigh bones—of a fairly large tropical ape.

Dubois' find rocked the anthropological world. It provoked so many arguments and such widespread disbelief that he eventually locked up his specimens and refused to let other scientists see them. Over the years he became increasingly suspicious and eccentric, and it was only in the 1920s that anthropologists could make a proper examination of Dubois' treasures, even though few scientists still doubted that these fragments were the oldest human remains discovered up to that time.

Following Dubois' finds, other remains similar to those of Java man were found: a good many in a huge cave near Peking, China; another one south of Peking; a couple in Java; more in Algeria and eastern Africa;

DRAFTSMAN
The draftsman charts both the vertical and horizontal position in the ground of every object that is found, so that later workers will know exactly where each piece came from when they study it later on.

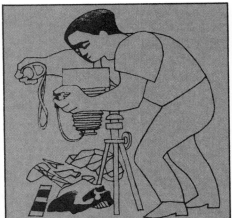

PHOTOGRAPHER
This man takes pictures of the fossils as they are found so that later workers will know how they were arranged, and so other people can see them when a report of the expedition is published.

PREPARATOR
As each fossil is found the preparator preserves and protects it with hardening agents such as epoxy, then gets it ready to be shipped safely to a laboratory where it will be studied further.

one near Heidelberg, Germany; and one in Hungary. But the close relationship between these different types of early man was not recognized at first and is, in fact, still being argued about. It is natural among discoverers of dramatically ancient fossils—and these fossils appear to be about half a million to more than a million years old—for each man to think he has hit on something entirely new. For a long time there was a "Heidelberg man," a "Peking man," a "Java man," each given its own Latin name as well. The skeletal parts of these ancient peoples were often very fragmentary, and methods of evaluating them were still inadequate. Only in the last decade or so have scientists become convinced that all these widely scattered fossils represent *Homo erectus*, a single human species.

The discovery of *Homo erectus* led to a very puzzling question: what sort of people came before him? There was an immense gap in man's knowledge, running back all the way to some possible ancestors known from fossils believed to be 10 to 20 million years old. Then in the 1920s an anatomist, Raymond A. Dart, announced another major discovery, this time in South Africa—a child's skull of a totally new type. Other finds later showed this to be a creature about four feet tall, apparently manlike enough to run about on the ground on hind legs, but apelike in some characteristics of skull and jaw. Dart christened his find *Australopithe-*

Studying Fossils in the Laboratory

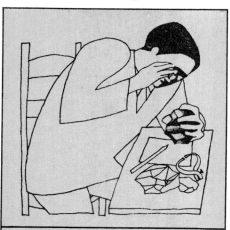

PETROLOGIST
After specimens are dug up, another team studies them in the laboratory. The petrologist, a rock expert, can tell what kind of stone was used, and whether the tools were made at the site where they were found.

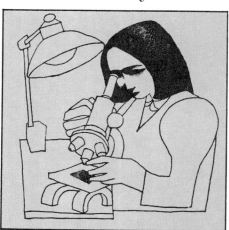

PALYNOLOGIST
A plant specialist studies grains of fossil pollen found at the site. This can help determine what plants were there at the time of early man and give clues to the climate and types of food available.

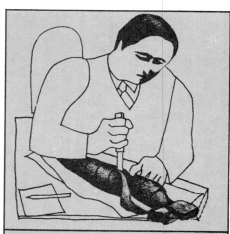

PEDOLOGIST
The pedologist studies samples of soil taken from the digging site. His information, along with the findings of the palynologist, can give a good overall picture of the plant life of early man's environment.

cus africanus. Since then, other African discoveries have been made, including a less primitive type that may have been the first hominid to make stone tools. The earliest of these pre-men lived some five or six million years ago!

One puzzling thing about the science of paleoanthropology (a word that is derived from the Greek for "ancient," "man" and "science") is the way important conclusions are drawn from the study of little bits and pieces. An entire head may be reconstructed from a patch of skull; a whole way of life may be pieced together from a few charred animal bones and some stone tools. How is this possible? The answer is complicated and much of the rest of this book will attempt to explain it. Almost all the sciences have contributed to paleoanthropology: botany, physics, biology, comparative anatomy and geology.

Today people realize that the earth is very old indeed. The problem now is to get accurate dates for human fossils, to figure out their relationships, to learn how they lived and to discover more of them.

Why can one find millions of shellfish fossils or thousands of reptile and mammal remains anywhere in the world, when people earlier than Neanderthal men are known from only a dozen or so sites? There are many reasons. First, many kinds of short-lived sea animals swarmed through the waters of the earth for millions of years, sinking to the bottom when they died, to

PALEONTOLOGIST
This man studies the remains of animals found near those of man. From them he can learn what animals the men may have hunted and eaten, and more about the kind of place in which they lived.

GEOCHEMIST
Using chemical and physical tests, such as potassium-argon and carbon-14 dating, the geochemist can often determine the exact age of the specimens that have been found at the digging site.

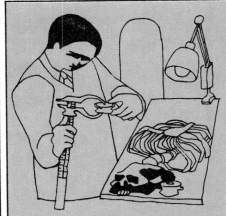

PHYSICAL ANTHROPOLOGIST
A specialist in the comparative anatomy of apes and men, this scientist studies the remains of early men to determine where in the overall evolution of man the particular bones belong.

be covered by sediment. Their way of life helped preserve them, as did their durable shells, the only parts of them that now remain. Men, by contrast, have never been as numerous as oysters and clams. They existed in small numbers. They were more intelligent than dinosaurs, for example, and were less apt to get mired in quicksand and tar pits, where their remains would have been nicely preserved. Most important, their way of life was different. They were lively, wide-ranging gatherers and hunters. They often lived and died out in the open, where their bones could be picked by scavengers, nibbled by ants, bleached and rotted by the sun and rain. Finally, men have only been around for two, or possibly

three, million years. They simply have not had as much time to scatter their bones about as the older types of animals have.

What is needed to catch a glimpse of early man is a cave where a corpse has been gently covered by dust, leaves or even sand and mud from the rising water level of a river. Or the cave can be a large one with a deep rock fissure that served as a garbage dump at the back, into which the dead were thrown along with the bones of game animals. Finally, the cave may simply be one that was occupied steadily for a long period of time. The dirt and mess of mere living gradually built up the floor, so that if people lived in the cave long enough, their story will be revealed by digging down

from one layer in the earth to the next.

Layers in a cave tell a rich story if they are investigated carefully and their evidence is read correctly. Earlier investigators often dug with reckless abandon, throwing shovelfuls of material every which way to recover only the largest bones and pieces of worked stone. They did not realize that the position of things relative to each other is important, as is chemical analysis of the surrounding earth itself. Many questions arise. Is there evidence of fire? Was the fire natural, or was it controlled by man? Are there more bones of certain kinds of animals at one level than at another, indicating a change of diet or climate? Do the deposits preserve pollen grains, which are clues to vegetation

Fossil-Finders' Painstaking Work

On expeditions to find the remains of early man and the animals he hunted, experts carefully perform a number of different tasks. In the photograph below, an expedition leader, François Bordes, carefully probes the ground with a small pick, a pan and a brush. At far left a worker accurately records the position of a new find on a map of the digging site. In the picture at center, two other workers prepare prehistoric elephant bones for shipment back to the laboratory. After hardening them with a preservative and bracing them with metal rods, they protect them with plaster.

and hence excellent indicators of the prevailing climate?

When this kind of study is made of a place where early man lived, it can be compared with studies of other such sites. There may well be similarities as well as contrasts between them, permitting an even better understanding and dating than was possible from one site alone.

Modern work at sites occupied by early man is time-consuming and demanding. The tools of today's field worker are not so much picks and shovels as surveyor's transits, dental instruments and small camel's hair brushes. Using such tools, it may take weeks to excavate a very small area. Every scrap of evidence is gently and patiently worked free, then mapped both horizontally and vertically; everything is recorded, everything labeled.

Does this "nit-picking" type of work mean that the great, exciting days of paleoanthropology are over? Not at all. It is true that the basic concepts are nailed down and there can no longer be the kind of absolute astonishment that greeted the geological time concepts of Lyell or the evolutionary concepts of Darwin. Nevertheless, these are exciting times for paleoanthropologists. The evidence is growing almost faster than it can be analyzed. Each fact, each new discovery, speeds up the process of understanding. That is what is so thrilling about paleoanthropology today.

The highlights of this search for man's beginnings will be dealt with in the following chapters of this book. First we will consider what is known about the fossil apes and their possible connections with the fossil near-men, and then we will take a look at the near-men themselves, the australopithecines. They will be followed by *Homo erectus* and *Homo sapiens*. Among the latter we will study the lives of Neanderthal man, that Ice Age hunter of large animals; then Cro-Magnon man, both hunter and great cave painter, who lived just over the hill from us in time and was really no different from us physically. Finally, we will visit some Stone Age people who are still walking the earth today. Many of these people still practice a very primitive way of life that would be quite familiar to their ancestors of the distant past, 20,000 or 30,000 years ago.

An Old Shelter for Man

The cliffs of Laugerie Basse in southern France shelter a neat little village today, just as they have been sheltering humans for the last 30,000 years. This area of France was densely inhabited by both Neanderthal and Cro-Magnon peoples. Fossil hunters have often come here to study them.

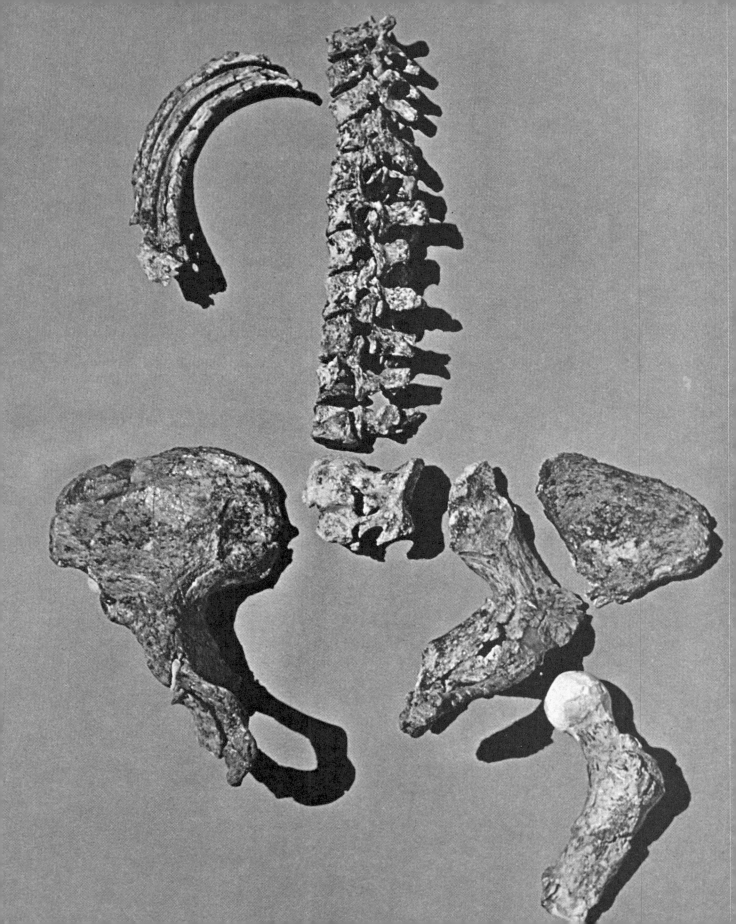

2

The Earliest Ancestors of Man

A FEW BONES—pieces of spine, hip bones and ribs—do not look like a big enough collection from which to reconstruct a whole body. But from these bits of an *Australopithecus africanus* scientists have figured out his approximate height and weight, and also the fact that he walked upright.

Once the idea of evolution is accepted, man's origins can theoretically be traced back 3.5 billion years to the origin of life itself. For practical purposes, however, the starting point is when he began to have the first faint traces of "mannishness." How far back to look for such traces, and even what to look for, is a problem. It was first stated by Huxley a century ago: "Was the oldest *Homo sapiens* pliocene or miocene, or yet more ancient? In still older strata do the fossilized bones of an Ape more anthropoid, or a Man more pithecoid than any yet known await the researches of some unborn paleontologist?"

An ape more anthropoid (manlike); a man more pithecoid (apelike)—that seems to sum it up neatly, but it does not go back far enough. To tell the story properly, we must look behind apes to monkeys and to the animals from which they sprang, because traits that would later emerge as human probably had their origins in the shapes and behavior of these creatures.

As we start our search we know only one thing: we know what we are like. It is as if, in a jigsaw puzzle, we have only the top edge (ourselves) fastened together. Below that we hope to fit in other pieces. For the pieces at the very bottom edge of the puzzle of man, we begin with the first hints of primates: the group to which monkeys, apes and men all belong. This takes us back about 70 million years to the Paleocene epoch, when human ancestors still looked more like squirrels than people.

The Paleocene era opened on a warm and placid world, with enormous tropical forests spreading much farther north and south from the equatorial belt than they do today. France and Germany had a moist, jungle climate; presumably, Africa and Asia were not very different. Among the inhabitants of these forests were many little animals called prosimians that resembled the tree shrews and tarsiers we know today.

They had paws to use for grasping tree limbs, and they were probably skilled at leaping about in the trees, and at finding fruit and seeds, insects and birds' eggs. What on earth did they have in common with us? At that point in time very little—yet many of them sat upright and their brains were already larger than the brains of their shrewlike relatives.

They also had a tendency to hunt with their eyes as well as their noses. Holding and looking, it turned out, were extremely important to the prosimians. As these traits developed, their eyesight improved, their eyes working around to the fronts of their heads until their depth perception was very

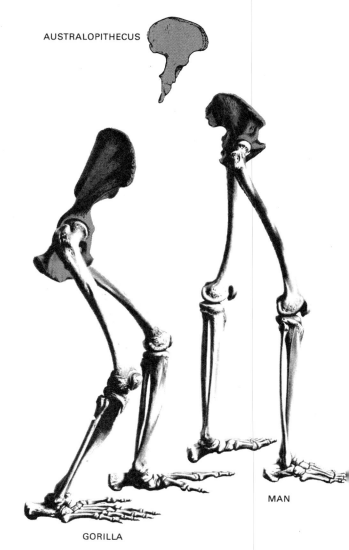

AUSTRALOPITHECUS

GORILLA

MAN

Changing Pelvis Shapes

The shape of an animal's pelvis has a lot to do with whether the animal can walk upright or not. The gorilla's pelvis is large and long and prevents the animal from standing up straight. In *Australopithecus*, and in man, the pelvis is shorter and its blades broader, allowing them to walk upright. The broad, curved portion projecting to the rear acts as an anchor for the large buttock muscles needed for standing, and makes the pelvis into a kind of basket that supports the body.

keen indeed. This, in turn, encouraged a more and more precise handling of objects, and improved the chances that these small creatures would survive. As tree-dwellers, they lived or died depending on their ability to judge distance and direction.

These were the early primates. Enough of their fossils have been found to show that many of them were not very different from several prosimians that still survive. For 30 or 40 million years prosimians were tremendously successful in the tropical forests, and during that time they began to produce a variety of types that were increasingly like monkeys or apes. In the process, most of the earlier types died out; today's prosimians are much reduced in both number and variety from those of the past, and most scientists agree that the later-model monkeys—bigger, stronger, better coordinated, and above all much more intelligent—have largely taken over from them.

It was not until the late Eocene epoch, about 40 million years ago, that anything even vaguely like a monkey showed up. What appeared then was a creature named *Amphipithecus*, a small piece of whose jaw has been found in Burma. In some respects, the jaw fragment indicated that *Amphipithecus* could be on the monkey line; but it is very difficult to tell from such a small and ancient fossil.

For a better clue we have to move ahead 10 million years to the Oligocene epoch to a sharp dip in the Egyptian desert approximately 60 miles to the southwest of Cairo.

This area is known as the Fayum Depression. It is one of the driest places in the world today, but in Oligocene times the Mediterranean reached this far inland and the Fayum lay between sea and forest, with tropical rivers emptying into the sea along it.

The Fayum contained a rich deposit of early primate fossils; not of the little prosimians that were so common in other regions at that time, but of creatures that were beginning to look more like monkeys. Among them were two that bear the names *Apidium* and *Parapithecus*.

What is it that makes *Apidium* or *Parapithecus* seem like an ape or a monkey instead of a prosimian? This gives us the first chance to see how the paleontologist can deduce so much from but a single piece of fossil evidence. Frequently, the main evidence is teeth.

Being the hardest substances in the body, teeth last the longest. As a result, more teeth than bones have been found, and teeth have been more closely studied. Anatomists have learned, for example, that animals have their own particular patterns of bumps, or cusps, on the tops of their molars (the grinding teeth in the back of the mouth). Old World monkeys have four cusps, which are connected in pairs by small ridges; prosimians do not. *Apidium* and *Parapithecus* have such teeth, but does that make them monkeys? Not really, for other parts of their mouths are more prosimian than monkey.

But comparative anatomists try to find

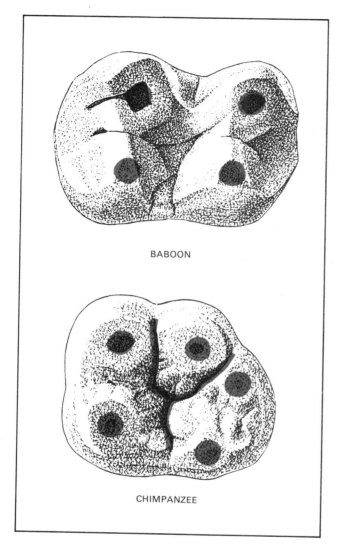

BABOON

CHIMPANZEE

A Message in Teeth

Frequently, a single tooth can indicate whether its owner was an ape, a monkey or a man. The molars, or back teeth, of Old World monkeys like baboons have four points (*color*), linked by two ridges. The lower molars of man and of apes, like the chimpanzee, have five points with a Y-shaped valley (*colored line*). This pattern varies in different species, but basically it has stayed the same for 24 million years.

other things that all monkeys have in common and that at the same time separate them from all other animals. Each genus of living animals has its own composition of characteristics, and how closely one genus, or one species, overlaps with another will determine how closely they are related. For example, dogs and wolves, which are different species of the same genus, look very much alike and behave in similar ways. They have so many characteristics in common that anyone can see that the two animals are very closely related. In the same way, both dogs and wolves share with cats the traits of four-leggedness, warm-bloodedness and sharp-toothedness as well as a great many others, but they are less like cats than they are like each other.

By systematically putting together the most minute bits of fossils, the paleontologist begins to get a pattern of relationships among long-extinct types. His evidence may be very scanty, but each new fragment either increases the similarity of one animal to another or decreases it. And as the bits of evidence are sorted out, enough characteristics such as bilophodontism may finally be nailed down for an expert to state with conviction, "Yes, this one is a monkey or a direct monkey ancestor, while that one is something else."

From this kind of detective work, it has been decided that *Parapithecus* and *Apidium* probably are not far removed from the main monkey line. In addition to teeth, there is another piece of "monkey" evidence: a frontal bone. This is one of the bones that come down around the sides of the eye to give the human skull its vacant stare. Among lower kinds of animals, the bones have not come together, but they have in *Apidium* and *Parapithecus*.

Was either one of these a direct ancestor of man? Almost certainly not. For one thing, some of the primates scampering around in the Fayum were more apelike than monkeylike. This is another way of saying that they were more manlike.

When the principal differences between apes and monkeys are spelled out, the "mannishness" of apes is unmistakable. The most obvious differences are in the trunk skeleton, reflecting the fact that monkeys are built to go on all fours and do so most of the time, and that apes by contrast tend to be upright. An ape's spinal column is shorter and stiffer than the spinal column of a typical monkey. The ape's pelvis is enlarged and broadened to support the weight of its body over its legs. Its head is balanced more or less on top of the spinal column rather than being thrust forward like a monkey's—and its brain is larger.

In sorting out the Fayum fossils, it would be helpful to have spinal columns and leg bones to aid us in identifying any apes or pre-apes that might be among them. Unfortunately, there is no such evidence, but, again, we do have teeth to study. We have seen that certain molars in Old World monkeys have four cusps. Among apes—and

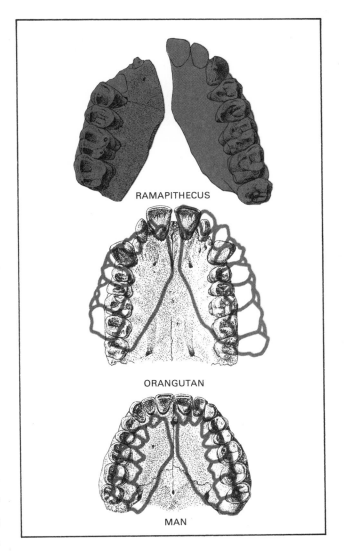

RAMAPITHECUS

ORANGUTAN

MAN

A Clue from Jaws

Fragments of the upper jaw of *Ramapithecus* show that he was manlike. One sign is that the canines, or pointed side teeth, are small compared to those of an ape like the orangutan. Also, the hard palate —the bony part behind the teeth—curves outward. When this jaw is placed over the jaw of an ape (*color, center*), and of a man (*bottom*), one can see that the *Ramapithecus* palate is very much like man's.

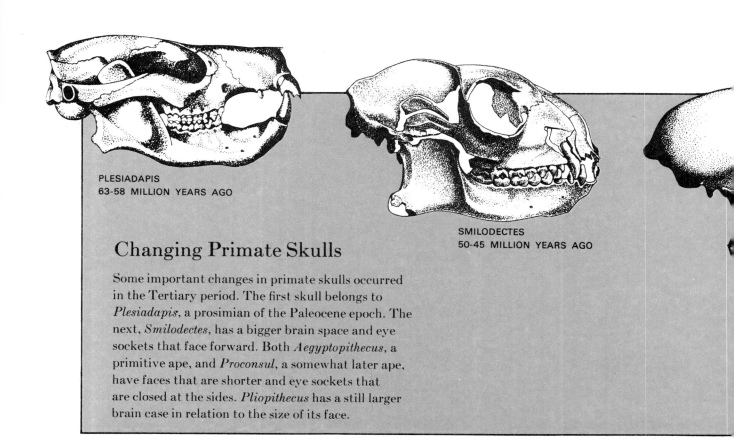

PLESIADAPIS
63-58 MILLION YEARS AGO

SMILODECTES
50-45 MILLION YEARS AGO

Changing Primate Skulls

Some important changes in primate skulls occurred in the Tertiary period. The first skull belongs to *Plesiadapis*, a prosimian of the Paleocene epoch. The next, *Smilodectes*, has a bigger brain space and eye sockets that face forward. Both *Aegyptopithecus*, a primitive ape, and *Proconsul*, a somewhat later ape, have faces that are shorter and eye sockets that are closed at the sides. *Pliopithecus* has a still larger brain case in relation to the size of its face.

men—these same molars in the lower jaw have five cusps, which are arranged in a Y-shaped pattern. Such teeth—and their jaws—have been found among the Fayum fossils. The first belong to an animal named *Propliopithecus*, others found later belong to a primitive ape, *Aegyptopithecus*.

The existence of monkeylike lower molars in some of the Fayum fossils and apelike teeth in others makes one startling fact plain: as long ago as 30 to 35 million years, the creatures that were becoming monkeys and the creatures that were becoming apes were already different.

Although the lower jaw of the *Propliopithecus* fossils gave a hint of the jaws of apes—or their ancestors—with the characteristic five cusps, it was the closely related

Aegyptopithecus that nailed down the existence of ancestral apes in the Oligocene epoch. The *Aegyptopithecus* fossil consisted of almost a complete skull, including an upper and lower jaw and nearly all the teeth. The canines from the upper jaw fitted the gaps in the lower jaw to provide their owner with the same slicing ability in chewing that modern apes have.

But even though this animal was clearly on the way to becoming an ape, its link with the past, and with monkeys, was still close. *Aegyptopithecus* is, in fact, the most primitive ape discovered, with a skull shaped very much like that of a monkey. The animal was the size of a spaniel, and in life it may even have looked more like a monkey than an ape.

Nevertheless, its jaws and teeth show that

28

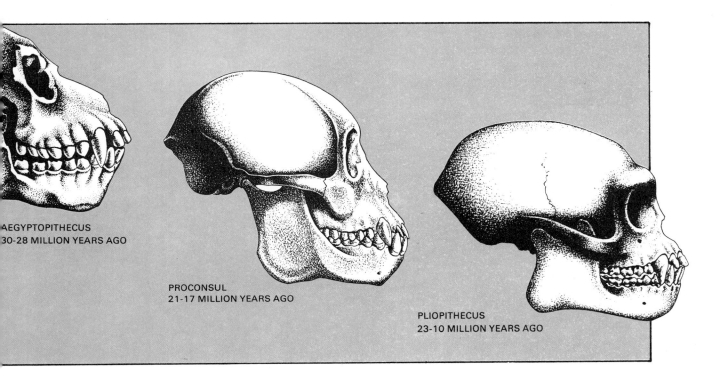

AEGYPTOPITHECUS
30-28 MILLION YEARS AGO

PROCONSUL
21-17 MILLION YEARS AGO

PLIOPITHECUS
23-10 MILLION YEARS AGO

Aegyptopithecus had moved from the monkeys onto a course of its own. Whether that course led to man is impossible to say. Some scientists believe that *Aegyptopithecus* had already become too much of an ape to have been man's ancestor.

Other evidence from the Fayum Depression indicates that not only were monkeys and apes distinct at that early date, but apes were beginning to differ from one another. There were little ones suggesting gibbons, larger ones that are probably ancestral to the modern great apes—and maybe more. Of the four kinds of apes—gibbon, orangutan, gorilla and chimpanzee—the gibbon is considered to be the least like humans; and, as Huxley described, the chimpanzee and the gorilla are most like humans. Therefore,

if we could find a chimpanzeelike or gorillalike fossil, we should have something close to ancestral man.

By jumping forward 10 million years or so in time to the Miocene epoch, we do find such creatures. One of them is *Dryopithecus*, whose many members were widespread in Europe, Africa and Asia 15 to 20 million years ago. Fossils of dryopithecines have been around for more than a century. Although they intrigued scientists, their importance was not fully appreciated until a strange fossil, later called *Proconsul*, was discovered in the 1930s on an island in Lake Victoria in East Africa. *Proconsul*'s resemblance to the chimpanzee was quickly recognized, but the creature also had monkeylike characteristics. What is more, in its face,

Creatures That Led to Modern Man

The stages in man's development from an apelike ancestor to the modern human being are shown in drawings on this and the following three pages. Some of the stages have been drawn on the basis of very little evidence—a few teeth, a jaw or some leg bones. However, experts can often figure out a great deal about what a whole animal looked like from studying these few remains.

In general, man's ancestors have grown taller as they became more advanced. For purposes of comparison, this chart shows all of them standing although the ones on this page actually walked on all fours.

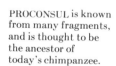

PLIOPITHECUS, one of the proto-apes, looked much like a modern gibbon and is often classed as its ancestor.

PROCONSUL is known from many fragments, and is thought to be the ancestor of today's chimpanzee.

DRYOPITHECUS was the first fossil great ape to be found. Its remains have been found in Europe, Asia and Africa.

OREOPITHECUS was once thought to be an ancestor of man, but is now thought to be a possible side branch on the family tree.

jaw and teeth were traits that could even be considered manlike.

Could this be the first whisper of humanity? In the excitement surrounding the *Proconsul* findings, scientists began to study *Dryopithecus* again. Seen with new eyes, it quickly came into focus. It is the same kind of creature as *Proconsul*.

Now a new puzzle appeared. An increasingly large number of *Proconsul* fragments were being put together, and they indicated

that the animal appeared in more than one size. Not only does one seem to have been the ancestor of chimpanzees, but a larger type may be the ancestor of modern-day gorillas. Whatever their size, *Proconsuls* are now grouped as dryopithecines.

With pre-gorillas and pre-chimps around, we are close to the ancestral human line. Can we place any of the *Proconsuls* or other dryopithecines on this line? So far, we do not have enough fossil evidence that points to

RAMAPITHECUS is thought to be the oldest of man's ancestors in a direct line, although only a few fragments have been found.

AUSTRALOPITHECUS AFRICANUS is probably descended from *Ramapithecus*. He walked on two legs.

AUSTRALOPITHECUS ROBUSTUS was a more recent species than *africanus*, and was a dead end in evolution.

AUSTRALOPITHECUS BOISEI was the largest of the australopithecines. He lived in eastern Africa.

one member leading to man. Furthermore, as more and more fossils are found, man's ancestral picture becomes more and more complicated. We now know that there were a number of animals living 8 to 15 million years ago that could have been the ancestors of man and near-man.

The one usually considered to be a direct, if distant ancestor is *Ramapithecus*, identified in the 1930s by G. E. Lewis of Yale University. During an expedition to the Si-walik Hills in India, Lewis obtained part of a jaw with a few teeth attached that he recognized belonged to a distinct manlike kind of animal. Monkeys and apes have flat palates and jaws that form a U shape. *Ramapithecus* had an arched palate as humans have, and its shape indicated that the jaw would have the shape of a V, widening at the back. Lewis classified *Ramapithecus* a hominid (on man's line). Other scientists, however, were not ready to accept this classification. Besides,

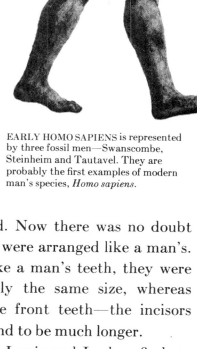

HOMO HABILIS, an adept tool user, was more intelligent than his cousins. He was a neighbor of *boisei*.

HOMO ERECTUS was the first man of our own genus, *Homo*, to be found in widespread areas. He had modern limbs, but a more primitive brain. He lived in groups and knew the uses of fire.

EARLY HOMO SAPIENS is represented by three fossil men—Swanscombe, Steinheim and Tautavel. They are probably the first examples of modern man's species, *Homo sapiens*.

there was another wide-jawed fossil around called *Bramapithecus* that was known only by a lower jaw.

Nothing much happened for a quarter of a century. Then anthropologist Louis B. Leakey discovered in Africa an upper jaw that closely matched that of *Ramapithecus*. This jaw was chemically analyzed and found to be 14 million years old. From these two finds a pretty good upper jaw with all its teeth could

be reconstructed. Now there was no doubt that these teeth were arranged like a man's. Furthermore, like a man's teeth, they were all approximately the same size, whereas among apes, the front teeth—the incisors and canines—tend to be much longer.

Matching the Lewis and Leakey finds to form one good *Ramapithecus* jaw was suggested by Elwyn Simons of Yale University, and he pushed the identification of the two as a single species (even though one came

NEANDERTHAL MAN was not such a brute as many people think. He had a skull capacity in some cases bigger than that of modern man, and he made a variety of tools of advanced design.

CRO-MAGNON MAN replaced Neanderthal man in Europe. Only a cultural step away from modern man, he left the world cave paintings and stone carvings that are now famous.

MODERN MAN is physically very much like Cro-Magnon man. The difference between them is cultural. In learning to grow food and domesticate animals modern man became settled and civilized.

from India and the other came from Africa). To strengthen *Ramapithecus'* credentials, Simons searched through fossil collections for clues that might have been overlooked. He wondered why one of the only two curve-jawed types (*Ramapithecus*) was known only by upper jaws, and the other (*Bramapithecus*) only by lowers. It occurred to him to put the jaws together. They fitted—*Bramapithecus* and *Ramapithecus* were one and the same. The name *Bramapithecus* was dropped

from the list and *Ramapithecus* now had both an upper and a lower jaw. His credentials as man's oldest known direct ancestor had advanced another step.

Recently, new discoveries have further strengthened *Ramapithecus'* claim. The most exciting of these finds is a complete, undistorted lower jaw with either the crowns or sockets of all the teeth. This was found in India's Siwalik Hills in the mid-1970s by an

(*Text continued on page 36*)

North America

South America

EARLY APES

AUSTRALOPITHECINES

HOMO HABILIS

HOMO ERECTUS

EARLY HOMO SAPIENS

NEANDERTHAL

CRO-MAGNON

EXTENT OF GLACIERS

Where Man's Ancestors Lived

This map shows the areas (*marked with skulls*) where different ancestors of man have been unearthed. The key, arranged in chronological order at left, identifies them. Early apes ranged widely over Africa and Eurasia, while australopithecines, who came next, have been found only in southern and eastern Africa, and in Indonesia. Remains of early *Homo sapiens* have been discovered mostly in Western Europe as have those of Neanderthal and Cro-Magnon man, who were so adaptable that they could live in the cold right at the edge of glaciers. Most of their remains have been found in the north.

35

international team headed by Dr. David Pilbeam of Yale University and Dr. Ibrahim Shah of Pakistan. Judged to be approximately 10 million years old, the jaw is V-shaped and both the front teeth and the canines are small—all very encouraging for hominid status.

Anthropologists are eagerly awaiting the next *Ramapithecus* find, if it should come. They are also, like Simons, taking some second looks at the bones now in museums. As more and more of this rechecking goes on, the Miocene primate picture can only become clearer. There are many pithecuses that have not been mentioned in this necessarily brief chapter—*Oligopithecus*, *Oreopithecus*, *Aeolopithecus*, *Limnopithecus*—to name just a few. Most of these creatures exist only in fragments, and which fragment belongs with which is still being figured out.

What they do make clear is that the primate tree had no large central trunk, but was more like a luxuriant vine with many shoots and tendrils growing side by side, sometimes withering and dying, sometimes branching. And in those branches we see the extremely ancient prosimianlike types, the more advanced monkeylike and apelike types, and finally a group that belongs definitely in the ape line alone.

The 10 million years of the Miocene epoch, then, saw the development of a number of proto-apes. They were widely distributed through Europe, Asia and Africa; they were evolving rather rapidly; and they probably were very numerous. Toward the end of the Miocene epoch, about 14 million years ago, one of them, *Ramapithecus*, began to show unmistakable hominid traits. Until a better candidate comes along he may be considered the ancestor of man.

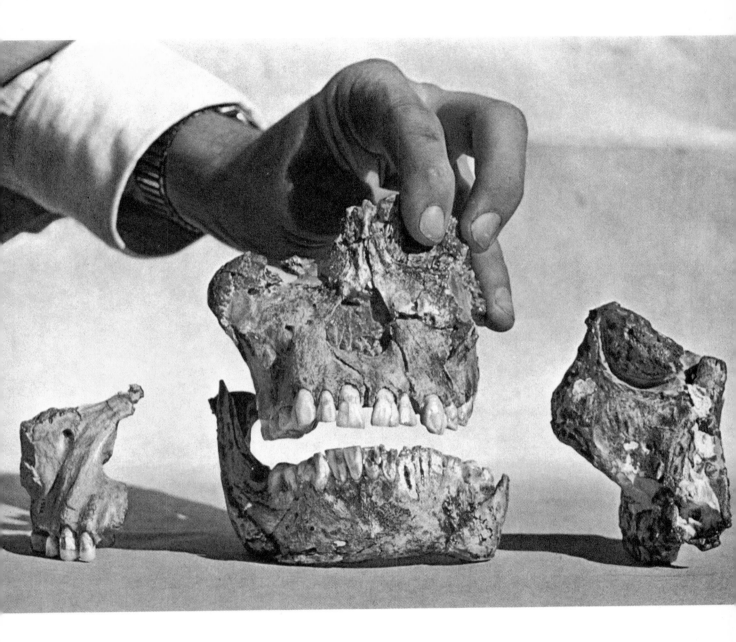

Jaws That Resemble Man's

The jaws of *Australopithecus*, some two million years old, look more human than apelike. This fact helped convince scientists that the creature was one of man's ancestors. Like man's jaws, those of *Australopithecus* are relatively short from front to back, and the front teeth, or incisors, are small.

3
Trial and Error on Evolution's Road

AUSTRALOPITHECUS ROBUSTUS was one of the upright, two-legged creatures that evolved in Africa approximately two million years ago. He was small-brained and had heavy jaws and teeth. By half a million years ago *robustus* had become extinct, probably killed off by his near relatives.

Sometime after *Ramapithecus* lived, new kinds of primates began to emerge, unlike any that had lived before. And they started to leave the forest for the open plains, moving upright on two legs.

The importance of two-leggedness cannot be overestimated. Apes and monkeys can move on two legs for short distances, but they are not really built for it. Man in contrast cannot function properly in any other way. Sometime during the Pliocene epoch at least one kind of primate began to walk on two legs and use tools, and developed a large, complex brain.

The first proof that such a creature existed came in 1924. Raymond Dart, a professor of anatomy in Johannesburg, South Africa, was investigating baboon fossils from a limestone quarry. Among them he found the cast, or mold, of the interior of a skull, but it was not like any baboon skull that Dart had ever seen. Its proportions were different, and it was larger, much larger. Dart then searched until he found a rock with a hollow into which the stone skull-cast fitted perfectly. Painstakingly picking away tiny bits of rock, Dart gradually revealed the face and most of the skull of a child five or six years old. He named it *Australopithecus african-us*, the South African Ape, stating that he stood "intermediate between living anthropoids and man."

Dart's find interested scientists in Europe, but they did not agree that he was manlike. As a result, the Taung child—as Dart's skull was called, after the place where it was discovered—was long a subject of skepticism.

But Dart stuck to his guns. One thing made him feel sure that his find was very manlike: the hole through which the nerves of the spinal cord passed through the skull to the brain faced almost directly downward. This indicated that the Taung child had carried his head over his spine like a rock balanced on top of a pole; in apes and monkeys this hole is near the back of the skull, matching the more horizontal position of the spine. Dart was certain that the Taung child stood fairly erect.

Dart continued to pick away at the tiny skull and at last separated the upper and lower jaws, which had been previously cemented together. What he found further strengthened his case. Although these were only the small teeth of a child, they were not basically different from those of a human child—less different, in fact, than they were from those of a young ape. One striking thing about them was that the front teeth, the incisors and canines, were relatively small. Apes have such big front teeth that their jaws are longer than human jaws. Ape jaws are also heavier. The Taung child has short, light, manlike jaws.

By this time Dart had an ally. A paleontologist working in South Africa, Robert Broom, examined the Taung child and was convinced that Dart was right. But there was no adult skull, nor any leg or pelvic bones to prove the erectness suggested by the child's spinal hole. Broom was not free until the 1930s to search for them. Then, from two new South African fossil sites, he recovered enough fragments to piece together several almost complete adult skulls. He found other body bones and parts of a pelvis that confirmed that their owners had stood upright. All this evidence fitted Dart's original concept of *Australopithecus*, but the individuals from the sites were not quite alike. Apparently more than one kind of erect pre-man had once wandered about South Africa.

But why did these australopithecine ancestors leave the lush forests for more open country? They almost certainly came down from the trees for food.

Toward the end of the Miocene epoch or early in the Pliocene epoch a vast tropical forest spread over most of Europe, Asia and much of Africa. This means that there also was a large amount of forest edge, with opportunities for the tree dwellers to descend to the ground and eat the berries and roots that were plentiful in the open. Like many

(Text continued on page 45)

Tools Made from Leftovers

The bones and teeth shown here belonged to extinct animals that were probably eaten by *Australopithecus africanus*. Some experts believe that after a meal these early men saved leftover tusks *(left)*, leg bones *(center)* and teeth *(bottom)* for tools. They may have used these tools for chopping, cutting and scraping, and also as hunting weapons.

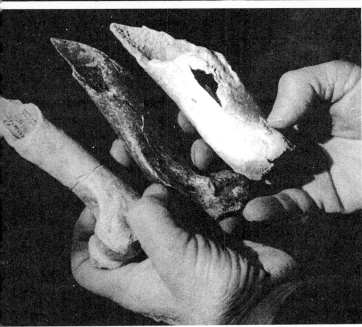

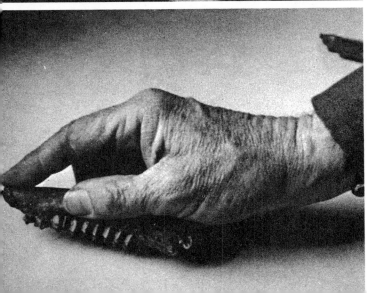

Life on a Peaceful Plain

Olduvai Gorge, where numerous fossils of early man
have been found, probably looked like this when
prehumans lived there. Periodically the volcanoes
in the background poured out lava, preserving some

of the inhabitants as fossils. Among the abundant wildlife were early antelopes and gazelles, a giant baboon and rhinoceroses (*left*), and a lumbering relative of the giraffe (*right foreground*). Lions, hyenas, and saber-toothed tigers fed on this game, as did several kinds of early hominids. Some of these pre-men are seen in the background building a ring of stones whose purpose is as yet unknown.

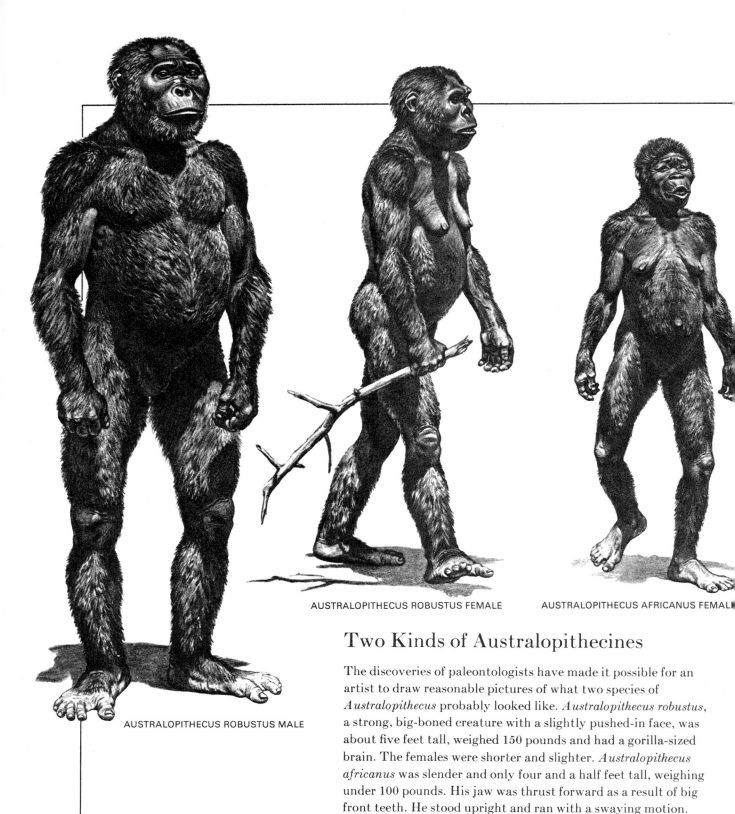

AUSTRALOPITHECUS ROBUSTUS FEMALE

AUSTRALOPITHECUS AFRICANUS FEMAL

AUSTRALOPITHECUS ROBUSTUS MALE

Two Kinds of Australopithecines

The discoveries of paleontologists have made it possible for an artist to draw reasonable pictures of what two species of *Australopithecus* probably looked like. *Australopithecus robustus*, a strong, big-boned creature with a slightly pushed-in face, was about five feet tall, weighed 150 pounds and had a gorilla-sized brain. The females were shorter and slighter. *Australopithecus africanus* was slender and only four and a half feet tall, weighing under 100 pounds. His jaw was thrust forward as a result of big front teeth. He stood upright and ran with a swaying motion.

AUSTRALOPITHECUS AFRICANUS MALE

monkeys and apes today, some proto-apes undoubtedly came down to the ground occasionally to feed there. The process was so gradual, of course, as to be unnoticeable, except over great spans of time. No single decision by a single ape or group of apes had any importance. But where the ground provided a better living than the trees did, the apes that were best adapted to life on the ground spent the most time there, and as time went on their descendants were still better adapted—and so on.

The University of California's Sherwood Washburn makes a striking point about erect stance and tool using. Most opinions have been that erect posture came first, that it freed the hands to use tools. Washburn suggests that tool using came first, and even led to walking on two legs.

We should not forget that apes were able to stand even before they left the trees. Apes swung from branches, sat in them, and sometimes even stood on them. Their eyesight, brains and hands had already begun to develop. Chimpanzees, in fact, use tools today. They strip leaves off twigs and use them to dig. They carry these tools around and take them to their nests.

From here on, all is guesswork, but the guesses are very logical. The most useful way for a tool user to get about is on his feet, with the result that his hands are left free to carry things. Chance success with throwing stones and sticks may have led to the idea that rocks and clubs were useful as weapons. With these new weapons, their

Two Ways of Life

MEAT-EATING may have begun when early populations of *Australopithecus africanus* started picking over the remains of animals killed by larger animals. In this picture one man drags off an antelope head while others throw stones at hyenas, which are also trying to make off with some of the meat. Anthropologists think *Australopithecus africanus* ate meat because they have found smashed animal bones with his remains.

AUSTRALOPITHECUS ROBUSTUS was probably less of a meat-eater than *Australopithecus africanus*. In the scene at right, a male is shown reaching up for some pieces of fruit, while a female with a stick digs in the ground for edible roots. Some anthropologists think that *Australopithecus robustus* ate mainly roots and other tough vegetable material because he had huge grinding teeth and powerful jaw muscles.

owners could have ventured farther and farther from the sheltering trees. Eventually they could have become completely ground dwelling, with natural selection producing animals that were more and more skilled at running on two legs.

To a creature that uses tools, brain development becomes more and more important. Skull size and shape slowly changed, probably to provide more brain space. At this point two-leggedness, brain development and tool using are interlocked, each depending on and stimulating the others. As one develops, a faster development in another takes place, and in turn encourages a new development in the first. This "positive feedback" could well have produced *Australopithecus.* So apparently tools are vital. At any rate, if two-leggedness does depend on tool use, then it stands to reason that *Australopithecus,* who was unquestionably two-legged, must have been a tool user. But Dart and Broom found no stone tools with their fossils, a fact that made many scientists doubt their conclusions.

At first Dart and Broom were too busy puzzling over the two kinds of australopithecines that they had found to worry about tools. The first of these creatures was rather small—lithe, slender, and weighing no more than 80 to 100 pounds. Broom calculated that he was between one and two million years old. This was a very rough guess because little was known about the geology of

(Text continued on page 50)

47

A Prehistoric Battle Scene

One interesting possibility suggested by fossils at
Olduvai is that *Australopithecus boisei* and his
relatives, the advanced australopithecines, may
have met each other and had mock fights like

the one shown here. At left, two advanced australopithecines, holding tools they have made, face a group of *Australopithecus robustus* males, who prepare to fight with rocks, while their females run away. Probably such a meeting startled both sides but finally the advanced australopithecines, whose wits had been sharpened by hunting, may have helped kill off the *robustus* species.

the South African caves and quarries where these finds were made.

The second type of australopithecine fossil was found with the remains of more recent animals than was the small and graceful *Australopithecus*. He therefore had to be younger and presumably that much closer in time to true man.

But Broom soon discovered that this second type stood more than five feet tall and weighed perhaps as much as 130 to 150 pounds. His skull and jaw were massive, almost gorrillalike, particularly in the bony ridge on the top of his skull. Instead of being more manlike, he was more primitive.

How could a more primitive type occur so much later than a more advanced one? This question bothered not only Broom, but his assistant, J. T. Robinson, as well. By the mid-1950s, a total of five sites had yielded hundreds of examples of both creatures. In addition, geological studies made of the sites by another South African, C. K. Brain, were producing better evidence concerning their ages. A kind of order for australopithecines began to appear. *Australopithecus africanus* has proved to be the smallest and oldest. By contrast, the geologically younger one, named *Australopithecus robustus*, was large from the start and stayed that way.

No stone tools had been found in South Africa until Robinson and Brain recovered some in 1957. Fossil teeth that may have belonged to an australopithecine were found with the tools, but the remains were too incomplete for sure identification. Before this,

Louis Leakey and his wife Mary had found very ancient stone tools in Olduvai Gorge in East Africa, and named them Oldowan, but they had found no fossils of the creatures that made the tools.

Most of the Leakeys' finds were made in this miniature Grand Canyon in Tanzania. Its sides resemble a layer cake of different strata laid bare by an ancient river. Leakey took great quantities of fossils from beds that overlie one another from the bottom to the plain some 300 feet above. In the lowest deposits Leakey discovered a number of very primitive stone tools. They were hopelessly crude, but Leakey recognized that they had been chipped by some directing —if dim—intellect.

They were the oldest known implements in the world, but who had made them was a mystery for years. Not until the 1950s could the Leakeys begin systematic excavation of the Olduvai Gorge. The story of their first find of a manlike creature is dramatic. On July 17, 1959, Louis was in camp with a fever when Mary rushed in to say that she had found a hominid fossil. Leakey forgot his fever and tore back to the site. There, in Bed I, the lowest layer, was an unmistakable hominid face and teeth, together with primitive tools.

It soon became evident that the Leakeys' find was another robust australopithecine. But this one was superlarge—and even more primitive. As a result, he was classified as a new species: *Australopithecus boisei*. The

CATCHING A BUSHBUCK

The Early Hunters

Australopithecus africanus ate mostly vegetable matter, but he also probably scavenged animals' kills and even went hunting on occasion. He was cunning and knew the animals' habits. Above, two *Australopithecus africanus* men corner a bushbuck and bring it down, using no weapons. At right, australopithecines crack and twist antelope bones to get at the marrow. Later, the bones may have been used as tools and weapons.

CRACKING OPEN BONES

Using Simple Tools

In order to be able to hunt more efficiently, australopithecines may have invented simple tools like the ones pictured. At right, a male spears a porcupine with a dry, hardened branch from a thorn tree. Such naturally sharp objects were probably used long before man made weapons. Below, another male offers a hyrax he has killed to a female who is skinning a piglet with a crude stone tool.

SPEARING A PORCUPINE

BRINGING HOME THE KILL

extremely ancient robust type in a site full of tools bothered many scientists. They had felt that the graceful little *Australopithecus africanus* would surely be the toolmaker since his brain was relatively larger and he seemed to be more manlike than his robust relative.

In one dramatic stroke, Leakey disposed of this problem less than a year after *boisei* was found. A second skull was found in Olduvai near *boisei*'s remains. Leakey and his colleagues named it a new species—*Homo habilis* (handy man)—even though the skull was quite a lot like *africanus*'. Leakey quickly announced that *habilis*, not *boisei*, must be the tool user. By the time the new name was announced in 1964, remains of other such tool users had turned up, and Leakey had become convinced from studying them that *Homo habilis* not only was man's direct ancestor, but also was on a separate line altogether from all the australopithecines that had been found up to that date.

Trying to find out who man's ancestors were has become ever more baffling as new discoveries are made in East Africa and also in Ethiopia. Some of the discoveries fill in a period that had been a gap in our family history. One find may establish the small, graceful *africanus* in East Africa 5.5 million years ago. All that we have of this fossil is a piece of lower jaw, discovered by Professor Bryan Patterson of Harvard University near Lake Turkana (formerly Lake Rudolf).

F. Clark Howell, the author of this book, has found many traces of australopithecines along the Omo River in Ethiopia, not far from Lake Turkana. Some teeth of small australopithecines are at least 2.5 million years old. In certain ways, the teeth are like those of *Homo habilis*, but in others they more closely resemble the early *africanus* teeth from South Africa.

One discovery that was as confusing as it was amazing is a large 2- to 2.5-million-year-old skull found in Kenya by Richard Leakey, the son of Louis and Mary. Unearthed in fragments, the cranium, when fitted together, was found to have the amazing size of about 750 cubic centimeters, just within the range of *Homo erectus*. With the help of this skull, called 1470 after its Kenya National Museum registration number, Leakey set out to prove that early *Homo* lived at the same time as the australopithecines. He also hoped to establish that South African australopithecines should be excluded from man's ancestry.

Some of the most exciting new fossils that are helping to determine man's evolution have been found in Hadar, a remote area in northern Ethiopia. An expedition, led by French geologist Dr. Maurice Taieb and American anthropologist Dr. Don Johanson, has unearthed 3.5-million-year-old jaws that have tentatively been classified as *Homo*.

Taieb and Johanson have also discovered a hominid skeleton that is about three million years old. Enough major bones have been found to give, for the first time, a clear picture of the structure of an ancient hominid. Named Lucy, because the pelvis is that of a female, this one was about three and a half feet tall, and bipedal. Lucy had a primitive, V-shaped jaw with teeth that were tiny but whose proportions—large molars and smaller front teeth—are usually associated with the massive jaws of australopithecines.

Lucy is proving to be very valuable to anthropologists as they try to judge other African fossils. For the first time they see teeth, arms, legs and pelvis that belong together. But Lucy, as a primitive hominid similar to australopithecines, is important for another reason: she is a half a million years younger than the *Homo* jaws Johanson found. Is this more proof that *Homo* developed alongside the australopithecines? Johanson and Leakey think it is.

East Turkana has also produced a skull resembling that of a South African *africanus*. And this one is approximately the same age as 1470 man. Thus, at both Hadar and East Turkana there seems to be increasing evidence not only that *Homo* may have existed as far back as 3.5 million years ago, but also that at one time—perhaps for more than two million years—*Homo* and the aus-

tralopithecines did indeed live side by side.

Little by little, anthropologists are beginning to think that *Homo* and *africanus* have a common ancestor—in all probability a slight, graceful type like *africanus*. Furthermore, they think that Lucy may have been one of the late survivors of this ancestral group—and, as such, lived at the same time as more advanced relatives.

Figuring out who was what is difficult for many reasons. There is the question of the kinds of skull, teeth, limbs and pelvis that identify *Homo* and pre-*Homo*. Yet, for the moment, we can make a few decisions about who our ancestors were, or were not. We can, for example, be sure that neither *boisei* nor *robustus* was a direct ancestor of ours. Apparently they could not compete with the wiry little creature that is increasingly being recognized as *Homo habilis*. Human or not, he *was* handy. Like his relative *africanus*, he ate many different kinds of food and learned to use sticks, stones and clubs for hunting and for self-defense. As *habilis* grew more skillful, he became larger, smarter and bolder. The next thing after him is the first true man—*Homo erectus*.

A Controversial Child's Skull

This skull of a young *Australopithecus africanus* was taken from a quarry at Taung in Africa by Raymond Dart, an anatomist. It set off a great argument, as nobody else believed that the skull belonged to a manlike creature. Later, after adult skeletons had been found, the child's skull was accepted.

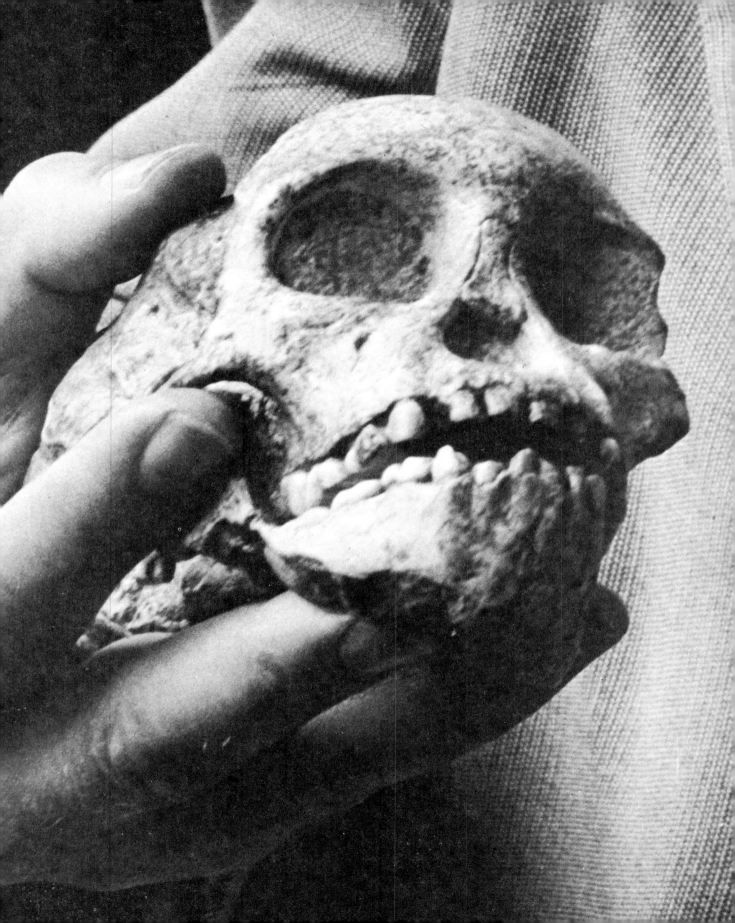

UNCOVERING A BOG, workers dig in the Ambrona
Valley in Spain. Although no human fossils have
yet been found, there is plenty of evidence that
Homo erectus made use of the bog. Heaps of elephant
bones and scattered tools indicate that he hunted
and butchered the beasts there.

4

Homo Erectus:
A True Man at Last

Fossil finds fall into two rough categories. There are the formerly unknown kinds that provide new insights into the evolutionary picture and there are those that add to what is known about a type already discovered. The first sometimes produces wild guesses and makes newspaper headlines. But the second, to the scientist, is often more important. For a clear picture of the characteristics of a species, one must have a series of fragments or skeletons from several individuals. Without such a series, a single fossil may be simply an exciting curiosity. It is the patient, less famous comparative studies of later finds that turn the wild guesses into scientific conclusions.

The story of *Homo erectus* is a splendid example of a wild guess that became respectable. When Eugène Dubois first turned up bits of an "ape man" fossil in Java back in the 1890s, it certainly made headlines. Ahead of its time, it faced a scientific world unready for it. It was by far the oldest and most primitive human fossil known. As a result, its apelike qualities were emphasized more than its manlike ones. Dubois gave it the name *Pithecanthropus erec-*

tus (erect ape man). But it was so unlike anything ever seen before that no one could agree whether it was a hominid or an ape.

This puzzling fossil became *Homo erectus*, now definitely known as an early species of man, as a result of many finds made since Dubois' discovery. Many anthropologists suspected the truth about Java man, and were impatient for new finds that might throw some light on it.

One such man was Davidson Black, a Canadian anatomy professor teaching in Peking, whose attention was drawn to a large cave in the limestone hills about 25 miles away from the city. This place was called Choukoutien by the Chinese, who had been digging fossils out of such spots for hundreds of years, grinding them up for medicines and magical potions. But some of the limestone caves were still richly packed with material when Black was shown two fossil teeth from one of them. On the basis of these two teeth, he persuaded the Rockefeller Foundation to sponsor an investigation of the area, under his direction.

Work began at Choukoutien in 1927, and within the year another tooth turned up. Struck by its size and cusp pattern, Black confidently announced a new genus of man —later to become known as Peking man and finally *Homo erectus*.

Over the next two years, tons of earth were excavated and, finally, a skull was located, encased in limestone. Black spent the next four months freeing it from the surrounding stone. When Black had cleaned the skull, he separated its bones, made a cast of each one and then reassembled the pieces. Now he could compare his find to Java man.

The two skulls matched in many respects. In each skull the bones were thick, the forehead low and sloping, with heavy ridges jutting out over the eye sockets. Black's skull was much more complete than Dubois', and for the first time Black could estimate the brain capacity of his find. It came to about 1,000 cubic centimeters, marking its owner definitely as a man and not an ape.

Black died in 1933, but his work at the site was carried on by Franz Weidenreich. In a decade, five skulls, nine skull fragments and 152 teeth were dug up. Particularly important were the remains of more than a dozen children, for a lot can be learned about a species by studying its growth patterns. Equally important, all the material came out of one cave with the order of the layers well preserved. It tells a vivid story about *Homo erectus* and the way he lived.

To begin with, the deposits are an astonishing 170 feet deep. They can be imagined by picturing an apartment building 17 stories tall, each story packed solid with blown-in dust and fallen plaster combined with rubbish left by its long-gone tenants. The trash of ages filled Choukoutien with layers of clay, of wind-borne soil, of limestone drippings, of fallen rock—all sandwiching other layers of human and animal remains. Large animals, too, occupied the caves; some levels contained the bones of big cats like the

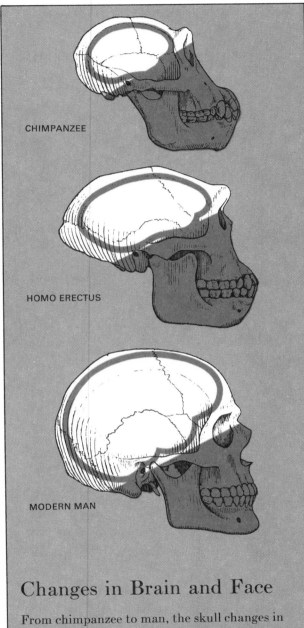

CHIMPANZEE

HOMO ERECTUS

MODERN MAN

Changes in Brain and Face

From chimpanzee to man, the skull changes in two major ways; the brain (*dark outline*) gets bigger and the face (*light shading*) gets smaller. *Homo erectus* falls almost exactly between ape and modern man. His brain space takes up about half of his skull. However, his heavy skull structure is more like that of an ape than a man.

saber-toothed tiger, as well as the remains of their prey. At other levels, it is clear that men drove the animals out and took over the caves. At first the animal and human layers alternate fairly regularly, but toward the top humans take over permanently. They left bones that vary in size from those of small rodents and bats up through bears, horses and camels to rhinoceroses and elephants— all told, some 60 species.

Certain levels are rich in tools roughly chipped of quartz or chert. They were obviously made by man, for they had to be brought from several miles away. Charcoal fragments and burned bones show up in many of the upper levels from which most of the human fragments have also been recovered, proving that *Homo erectus* used fire. He lived during times of bitter cold. Also, he was a vegetarian turned meat eater. He needed the help of cooking to digest the fats and proteins in his meat diet.

When and where man first learned to use fire will never be known. One of the earliest signs that he did so comes from Choukoutien, and dates back some 500,000 years. Probably he first borrowed burning twigs from brush fires caused by lightning, or he carried fire from volcanoes. Certainly these early fires must have gone out thousands of times before men learned to store fuel and how to keep fires going.

Possibly early man found out how to start a fire accidentally, while chipping flint tools. Sparks are frequently struck in this way, and they may have landed in dry leaves and begun to smolder. Cooking undoubtedly began through smaller accidents, when food fell into the fire and turned out to be tasty when it was pulled out. There is no way of proving any of this since behavior leaves no fossils. But *Homo erectus* was certainly intelligent enough to tame fire and to cook, and probably most of his kind used fire for much of their time on earth.

How long was this? Choukoutien tells us a good deal about *Homo erectus* himself, but it only hints as to where he came from, and of course says nothing at all about how and where else he might have lived. An obvious place to look for more evidence was Java, and there in the 1930s more fossils were discovered by the paleontologist G. H. R. von Koenigswald. Among them were fragments of five skulls. When one skull was put together, it was so much like Dubois' original Java skull that Von Koenigswald described them as looking like two eggs. Furthermore, when he and Franz Weidenreich compared the Java and Peking skulls, they decided they belonged to very close relatives.

Later, Javanese workers added to Von Koenigswald's specimens and found, along with tools for the first time, fossils much like some of the *Homo habilis* fossils at Olduvai. The fossils suggest that similar human populations existed one to two million years ago on both the east and west sides of the Indian Ocean—and probably around its coasts. But Africa is still the one place where *known* types from australopithecines to *Homo erectus* have been discovered and studied.

At Olduvai Gorge, *Homo habilis* existed alongside the giant *Australopithecus boisei*. There is also a fine example of *Homo erectus* that is about one million years old, as well as numerous fossils that have features of both *Homo habilis* and *Homo erectus*. Now Richard Leakey has found this remarkable succession of types at East Turkana. In 1975 he dug up a 1.5-million-year-old skull that he and other scientists quickly decided was a splendid example of *Homo erectus*. In fact, it is very much like Peking man.

Homo erectus must have been extremely successful, since his remains are so widely scattered about the globe. It is 8,000 miles from Olduvai by land around the Indian Ocean and down to Java. It is just as far from Olduvai to Peking. And *Homo erectus*— or a trace of him—also turns up in North Africa, Europe and the Middle East. How he came to live all over the Old World is not known. It is likely that the earliest form of *Homo* began to travel out of Africa and he evolved as he went—just as the stay-at-home developed into the first true man too. The travelers probably spread through the lush land corridor that stretched from Africa to Java, settling down for a few generations and then moving on, adapting not only to the hot, damp East Indian tropics but also to the bitter cold of northern China.

Physically, *Homo erectus* shows a considerable advance over *Australopithecus*, who could run well enough but probably walked poorly, waddling along on feet turned awkwardly out. *Homo erectus*, by comparison, was a superb walker. His legs were as long and straight for his height as modern man's. The females stood just under, and the males just over, five and a half feet. Choukoutien fossils show a broad flat nose, a low, sloping forehead, thick brow ridges and no chin to speak of. The head bones were thicker than a modern man's, the jaw was more massive. While the incisors and canines of the Mauer jaw found in Germany are within the range of modern man's, both the Mauer and Choukoutien molars are larger. The Choukoutien molars have an interesting cusp pattern that places them about midway between those of *Australopithecus* and *Homo sapiens*.

The size of the brain varied between 750 and 1,400 cubic centimeters, compared to 1,000 to 2,000 in modern man. As a general rule, apes and men share the same basic brain pattern. Certain parts are associated with certain functions. Toward the rear are areas that have to do with vision and information storage. In the center and at the sides are areas concerned with speech, memory, sensations and movements of the body. The front of the brain is where man does his thinking—and where an ape does whatever thinking it can. Sheer size in brains is important for two reasons: a small brain holds fewer brain cells than a large one, and the true quality of a brain depends on the complexity of the linkages between cells. Because the possible number of linkages rises very rapidly as the brain gets larger, a big brain can be much more complicated than a small one.

With their smaller brains, apes are limited in their activities. Their ability to communicate, for example, is below that of man. One chimpanzee has learned to ask questions and make her wishes known by pushing symbols that are part of a computer system; another has learned to "talk" with gestures of a recognized form of sign language. But with only a primitive vocal apparatus in its throat, no ape has been able to say more than a few words—and this is not speech in the true sense of communication. Man, however, with his well-developed physical equipment and more-advanced speech centers in the brain, has no such trouble.

To say whether *Homo erectus* could talk or not by examining his skull is extremely difficult, if not impossible. His brain was large enough to do most if not all of the things a modern brain can do. But we know nothing about the vital linkages inside. The shape of his brain was somewhat different from a modern man's. The central and side parts of his brain were smaller, but the speech centers and their connections were apparently in working order. Furthermore, recent studies of early man's vocal equipment indicate that, physically, he was capable of producing a variety of sounds. Developments in the organization of the inner brain encouraged physical changes in the vocal equipment, and vice versa. In due course, *Homo erectus* attained the power of speech.

We can learn somewhat more about the brain of *Homo erectus* from our knowledge of

Preparing for the Great Hunt

Above and on the following pages an artist has reconstructed
scenes of *Homo erectus* hunting elephants in the Ambrona
Valley. In this scene an old man watched by a boy sharpens a
hand-axe with a hammer made from an antler. The man by
the fire counts tools on his fingers, while two others wrestle.
At far right a hunter waits for others to join the group.

what he did. For one thing, he became a much better toolmaker and tool user than *Australopithecus* was. He progressed from the primitive chopping tool to a more efficient, if still crude, hand-axe. With his improved weapons he was a far abler hunter than *Australopithecus*, and could kill very large animals. This required planning and cooperation, which in turn meant that he must have lived in groups attached to a "home base." He had mastered the use of fire, and must have had some powers of speech; the ability to talk would have been essential to teach the young how to make his new tools, and it certainly would have been necessary to plan and carry out an animal drive—particularly one that involved setting grass fires to stampede a herd into a bog or over a cliff.

The idea that *Homo erectus* lighted fires to stampede animals is based on evidence found in a dry valley in north-central Spain. About 80 years ago a trench for a water pipe was dug in this valley, and many large animal bones were unearthed. An amateur archeologist, the Marqués de Cerralbo, later began serious excavations there. A paper about his findings fell into the hands of the author of this book, who decided the valley was worth studying and began work there in 1961.

The site, unlike the great cave at Choukoutien, promised to be an open-air residence. Few pre-Neanderthal human fossils exist in Europe, and the only good evidence at that time that pre-Neanderthal men lived there at all came from their widely scattered

stone tools. The trouble with stone tools is that they are often washed down into river beds along with gravel, and thus say nothing at all about the people who used them. This Spanish site was quite different. Studies of the area's layers, plus an analysis of fossil pollen, revealed that about 400,000 years ago the climate was going through periods of both warmer and colder weather than today. During the warmer times the landscape was more heavily wooded than it is now, but it was in a layer representing a cool, moist period that signs of man were first found. At that time, the valley where the villages of Tor-

ralba and Ambrona now lie was probably a migration route for animals ranging from deer, horses and wild cattle up to elephants.

The fossil sites at Torralba and Ambrona contained a huge number of elephant bones that belonged to an extinct, straight-tusked species somewhat larger than the African

The Fiery Hunt Is On

Homo erectus hunters used fire and mud to help them trap elephants. Here they drive a herd into a bog and set fire to the grassy bank at left to prevent escape. Already several animals are hopelessly stuck in the deep mud, including a big male that has fallen on its side.

Cutting Up the Giant Kill

At dusk, while the sky is still smoking after the drive, the
hunters butcher and eat the kill. The soft internal organs
are their first target, for they are easier to eat than the
tough outer flesh. One hunter squats, greedily gnawing a
morsel. Another *(right)*, carries a piece of meat out of the
swamp, walking on a crude bridge of cut-up elephant legs.

elephant of today. The bones were too numerous to have gotten there by accident. Besides, their condition and their position in the ground were extremely unusual. Many of the bones of the smaller animals, even some of the enormously heavy bones of the elephants, had been smashed open, presumably for their marrow. A large elephant skull had its entire top broken away. Most suggestive, the bones were all mixed up. The more these sites were studied, the clearer it became that somebody had been cutting up animals and dragging their bones around.

Mixed in with the bones were many signs of early man. Stone tools of a type associated with *Homo erectus* in Africa were abundant. There were also bone tools and even pieces of wood, pointed or flattened at one end.

Further, there was a quantity of material that showed different degrees of burning. This material was not so concentrated in any one place as to suggest hearths and continuous fires over a long period; it was widely scattered. Whoever lighted the fires burned grass and brush over large areas. The evidence, plus the elephant bones concentrated in what was then a bog, suggests that the fires were set to drive the elephants into the mud. Deep mud is usually fatal to elephants, and if the early men in the Ambrona Valley drove a herd of elephants into this bog, they could have killed the tuskers quite easily. It is hard to see how else so many large and dangerous animals could have been killed all in the same place. Nobody kills elephants and *then* drags them to one spot by hand.

Unfortunately, not a single human fossil has been found at either Torralba or Ambrona. We know that men moved in and out of these places, and we even know when they did. This dating, with the evidence of their tools, points strongly to *Homo erectus.* Still, it would be nice to nail all this down with just one skull.

Similarly, no fossils have been found at a site in Nice, France, called Terra Amata, though here there are also human footprints.

In general, *Homo erectus* may be labeled as a hunter, an extremely successful one at that. Apparently he was also a sociable fellow living in bands of 20 to 50 individuals, each band mixing with others and planning group hunts. Although he used natural caves for homesites, the camp at Terra Amata shows he built shelters with driftwood and saplings. Perhaps even more important was his move away from the tropics. As a result, he mastered fire, slept on animal skins and wrapped his body in them for warmth. He could talk and he could think. He was a doer and a planner. By the time he disappeared 300,000 years ago, he had set the stage for the entrance of modern man.

Dancing after the Hunt

Following the feast, one of the hunters drapes himself in the skin of a baby elephant and dances inside a ring of fire. Other men act out the hunt, leaping and pretending to throw spears, while the young children watch at left. In this way they learn about the hunt so they can take part when they grow up.

5
Skillful Toolmakers
of the Stone Age

A CLEAVER 10 inches long, and sharp, was one of the many effective tools that ancient man made out of stone. This one was found in Tanzania in Africa and was fashioned from a rock called mylonite. It was probably used by a Paleolithic hunter to cut up large animals into small pieces.

Lying row on row in the drawers of collections around the world are hundreds of thousands, possibly millions, of prehistoric stone tools. This may seem amazing compared to the extreme scarcity of fossils of the men who made them, and yet it is entirely logical. Stone is one of the most enduring substances on earth. And tools were almost always made of the hardest kinds of stone. Once made, they were practically indestructible.

Since the oldest stone implements known today are only between two and three million years old, practically all of the tools that have ever been made must still be lying around. It is no more surprising that so many have been found than it would be for some archeologist of the future to find Coca-Cola bottles that had been dropped one by one under a pier by a beach house.

Another reason there are so many stone tools is that each early man had only one skull to leave as a fossil, but he had a whole lifetime in which to make tools. He made them quickly, and when they grew dull or were lost, he made new ones. He started when he was a boy and continued throughout his life. So even among the australopithecine beginners in the tool business, one man might have made anywhere from dozens to hundreds before he died.

By the time of *Homo erectus*, man was much more dependent on tools, and, in general, he was making better ones. In some regions, however, man himself changed more than his culture. *Homo erectus* was still using the same tools in China, for example, that *Australopithecus* in Africa had used half a million years earlier, yet physically he had developed a great deal.

As the tool kits in other areas grew in number and variety, it is quite possible that a few members of a group would be named as the official toolmakers—perhaps because they were especially good at making tools or because they had physical handicaps that prevented them from hunting. This kind of specialization would have freed able-bodied men for other necessary activities. Furthermore, it would have been a logical part of the practice of dividing up various tasks among the more or less permanent members of a *Homo erectus* band.

The earliest recognizable man-made, man-used implement is called a chopping tool, or simply a chopper. Some choppers were as small as Ping-Pong balls, others as large as billiard balls. Most were made from roundish, smooth stones collected from stream beds or beaches. When used, such a stone, worn down to a round shape by the water, could be held firmly without hurting the palm. To turn it into a tool, two or three chips were knocked off one end with another stone. This gave it an edge of sorts or perhaps a rough point. These tools are readily recognized by an expert, but a more primitive tool might not be recognized by anybody since it would look just like a naturally pointed or edged stone.

Nevertheless, there are more primitive implements, and with luck and skill they can still be recognized. For one thing, large numbers of chips or flakes found in one spot show that tools were once made there. A stone that bears the marks of a great deal of banging and battering may have been used as a hammer or as an anvil. Finally, the presence of stones that do not normally occur at a site indicates tool use, even though the stones are not chipped. In fact, choppers are by no means the commonest kinds of tools found in these earliest sites. The small chips and naturally shaped stones are much more numerous. The latter, of course, were man's main tools for millions of years before it occurred to anyone to try to sharpen one himself.

A chopper probably was held as one would hold a rock while banging down at something with a direct hammering or chopping motion. Using a chopper in this way, *Australopithecus* was probably able to hack through animal flesh and sinews. The small, sharp chips that were knocked off in making choppers are called flakes. They were probably used for slicing and cutting.

A name like "chopper" describes a use that can only be guessed at by the archeolo-

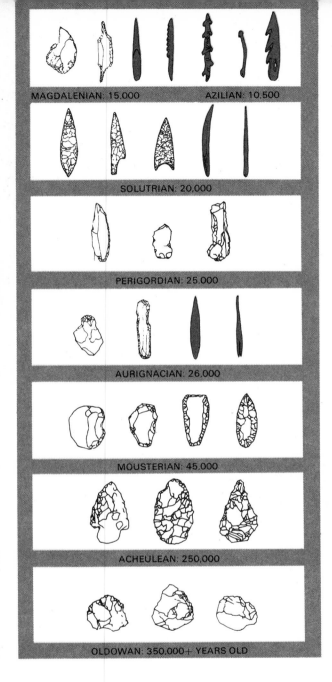

MAGDALENIAN: 15,000   AZILIAN: 10,500

SOLUTRIAN: 20,000

PERIGORDIAN: 25,000

AURIGNACIAN: 26,000

MOUSTERIAN: 45,000

ACHEULEAN: 250,000

OLDOWAN: 350,000+ YEARS OLD

The Evolution of Tools

The chart above shows how tools made by early European men developed over the ages. In the bottom row are three crude choppers at least half a million years old. Above this are later tools, with their ages in years noted below them. Implements made of bone are in color; the rest are stone. The delicate needles, points and harpoons in the top row were made by Cro-Magnon people in France.

gist. His guess may seem very logical, but it is still a guess. Several paleoanthropologists, among them J. Desmond Clark, Louis Leakey and S. A. Semenov, have tried to find a scientific basis for determining how tools were employed. They made several copies of a specific tool and used each copy in a different way—chopping wood, skinning animals, cutting flesh, scraping hides, digging roots. Then they examined the tools under a microscope to see if different uses produced different kinds of wear.

Besides being named after their use, stone tools are classified by types of workmanship in "industries," each named after the place where the type was first found. Thus the kinds of chopping tools that were discovered with *Australopithecus* remains in the Olduvai Gorge belong to the "Oldowan industry," no matter where else in the world they may happen to turn up.

All in all, the Oldowan industry lasted for at least a million and half years. How it left Africa and who carried it is not precisely known. Either *Homo habilis* or *Homo erectus* presumably spread the Oldowan industry through both Europe and Asia, but we have no positive identification of the exporter.

Only in 1963 was a fairly undamaged Oldowan site opened in Europe. This is Vértesszöllös in Hungary, and it became an extremely important one. Four levels occupied by early man have been found in thin layers, suggesting that he lived there for only brief periods of time. Some of the layers are mere scatterings of rubbish, but they contain burned objects, indicating the use of fire, a good many tools and the smashed bones of some 15 different species, mostly of small animals. The tools include many flakes and crude choppers simply chipped on one or two edges and primitive enough to qualify as Oldowan.

The tools at Vértesszöllös are much like those from Choukoutien. The curious thing is that along with such primitive tools were parts of a human skull that apparently belonged to a highly advanced *Homo erectus*. The site probably was inhabited from 500,000 to 250,000 years ago. It is one of the oldest known human occupation sites in Europe, since almost all the other sites contain signs of a more advanced tool industry.

This later style in toolmaking started more than half a million years ago. The principal style for several hundred thousand years throughout most of the world is called the Acheulean industry. The name comes from the town of Saint Acheul in northern France. The Acheulean seems to have spread rapidly from Africa into Europe and eastward as far as India. To understand the new style, one must know something about the ways in which stone can be shaped.

The ideal stone for a toolmaker is hard, smooth and fine-grained, for stones of this type shatter rather than crumble, and razor-sharp chips can be knocked off them. The best ones for early man were flint, chert and similar rocks. Flint was the most common in

How Stone Age Men Made Their Tools

CHIPPING one stone with another (*top drawing*) was one way Stone Age man made tools. When a chip (*dotted lines*) flew out, it left a sharp edge. Making a chopping stone from a round pebble is shown in views at right (*1, 2, 3, 4*). The toolmaker hit the pebble several times (*arrows*), to leave a ragged, sharp edge.

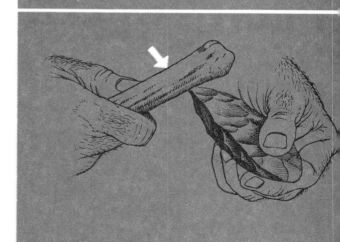

FINISHING THE EDGE of a tool, like the Acheulean hand-axe shown here, was done with a wooden or bone "hammer." By tapping the edge of the stone repeatedly with the softer instrument (*above*), the worker could strike off a number of chips. These left a sharp, fairly straight edge when the tool was finished (*right*).

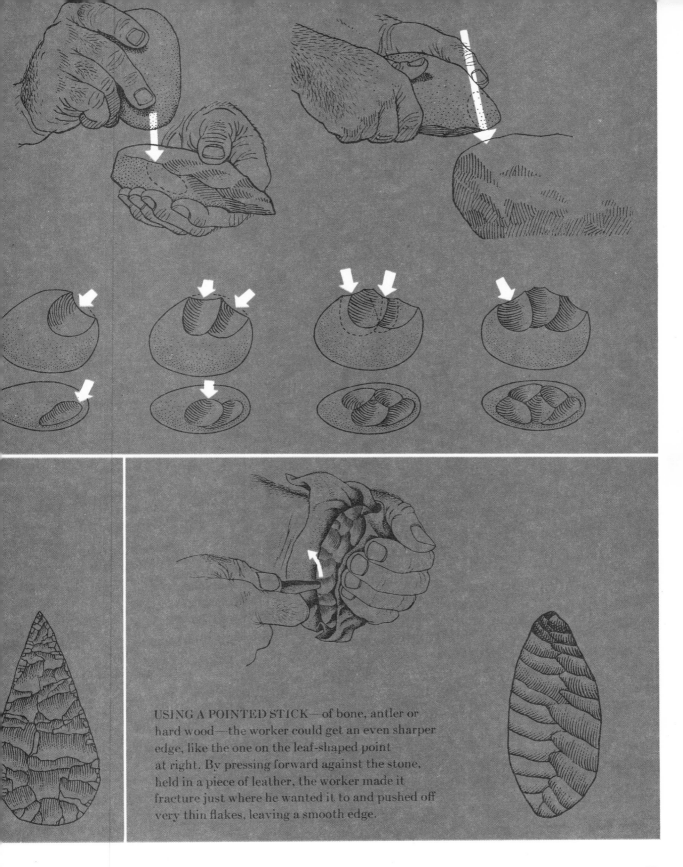

USING A POINTED STICK—of bone, antler or
hard wood—the worker could get an even sharper
edge, like the one on the leaf-shaped point
at right. By pressing forward against the stone,
held in a piece of leather, the worker made it
fracture just where he wanted it to and pushed off
very thin flakes, leaving a smooth edge.

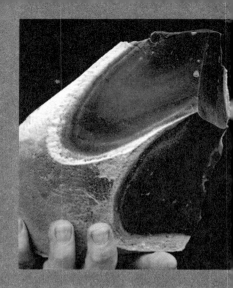

western Europe, and the typical Acheulean tool was a flint hand-axe. Where there was no flint, quartz, quartzite and other fine-grained rocks were used. Coarse granular rocks like granite are apt to crumble. Others are likely to break only along certain lines, so the toolmaker cannot control them.

The availability of good stone for tools helped determine where people lived during much of the Paleolithic period, and naturally many of their implements are found in or near rivers. Rivers are an almost endless source of pebbles and pieces of rock, and we should emphasize the word "pieces," for the best tool stone in the world was of no use to an early Stone Age man except in small hunks that he could shape.

The many kinds of stone and the various ways of working it produce a surprising variety of results. The more fine-grained the stone, the flatter and more leaflike the flakes will be. The size and shape of the flakes depend on the way they are made. They may be knocked loose by a direct hammer blow, or indirectly by placing a wood or bone chisel on the stone and striking the top of the chisel with the hammer. The angle of the ham-

A Professor Makes an Axe. . .

A French professor, François Bordes, is a leading
authority on Stone Age tools, and he is also an
expert at making them. In the pictures above, he
takes a piece of flint and knocks a few large chips
off it with a hammerstone. In the fifth picture he
switches to an antler hammer and chips both sides
of the edge to thin and sharpen it. The last picture
shows the finished axe, just like the ones Stone Age
men used for hundreds of thousands of years.

. . . and a Graceful Spearhead

In the pictures below, Professor Bordes takes one
of the large chips left over from making the hand-
axe and shapes a spear point out of it. He rests the
chip on his knee for support and starts chipping it
all over with an antler hammer (*second and third
pictures*). With the shape roughed out (*fourth picture*)
he starts to sharpen it by driving tiny chips from
the edge (*fifth picture*). When finished, the tool is a
perfect leaf-shaped point for a dagger or a spear.

mer blow can be changed to produce either a small thick flake or a large thin one. Also, different kinds of hammers produce different kinds of flakes. "Soft" hammers of wood or bone produce one kind and hard stone ones produce another. Even the way a tool is held while it is being made is important. When it is held in the hand the results are not the same as when it is balanced on a rock.

Stone is much more flexible than it seems, as you can see by experimenting with rocks yourself. If you live where flint or chert are to be found, you can discover that they are easily worked once you have developed some skill in handling them. The principles are described and illustrated in this chapter; with practice, you should be able to make your own simple tools.

You will not make them as fast and as well as François Bordes, the French prehistorian who can knock out a hand-axe in a few minutes. And you will certainly make nothing that *Homo erectus* would have been proud of. In fact, today's would-be toolmaker will learn to admire the skill of every ancient craftsman. This skill, of course, was based on necessity and years of practice. But the basic principles are fairly simple. It is surprising how a soft blow, struck at the right angle, can detach a big flake, and a hard blow, if struck at the wrong angle, will produce nothing more than a splinter.

In spite of all these techniques and materials, there are only two basic kinds or sources of tools: the "core" tools and the "flake" tools. To make a core tool, take a lump of stone and knock chips from it until it is the right size and shape: the core of stone that remains is the tool. A flake tool is a chip struck from a core.

In the earliest days of toolmaking, flakes were simply whatever happened to fly off a core. In general, flakes were used as cutters, or blades, because their edges were sharp, and choppers were used for heavy hacking. As time went on, more and more skills were developed in the manufacture of flakes, and eventually this became a much finer method of toolmaking than the core technique.

It was discovered that every flake struck from a core of a certain shape produced a long, bladelike flake with a straight and smooth cutting edge. A typical blade core was trimmed to a shape something like that of a very large strawberry, but with one flat surface. When a core of this shape was held point down and struck on its flat top, near the edge, a long knifelike splinter would fly off the side. If the core was turned a little and hit again, another perfectly formed knife blade was produced. The core was chipped down gradually, producing smaller and smaller blades until it was thrown away.

This technique was still practiced in historical times in Mexico, where obsidian, a hard black rock, is available from volcanoes. One observer watched a workman produce 100 usable blades in a little under an hour from obsidian cores.

As the Acheulean period progressed, core tools grew far more refined than the primi-

How Tools Were Used

Stone Age man made tools for many different purposes, and some of them are shown in the drawings on this and the next page. A primitive chopping tool could hack wood, crack bones and serve as a weapon. A polyhedral, or many-faced, stone, which was chipped all over, may have been used to smash bones and to bring down animals. Early hand-axes were useful for digging up roots to eat, while later axes with sharper edges were probably used for skinning and cutting up game. Sidescrapers were used to dress skins; they were easily made and are almost always found at sites where Neanderthal man once lived.

CHOPPING TOOL

POLYHEDRAL STONE

EARLY HAND-AXE

LATE HAND-AXE

SIDESCRAPER

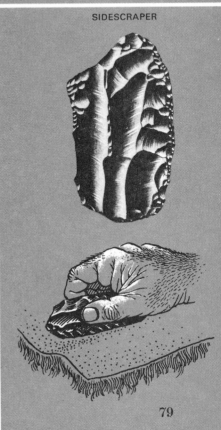

LEVALLOIS POINT

Specialized Tools

At digging sites where Stone Age man's remains have been found, there are many tools that seem to have been made with specific tasks in mind. A Levallois point with a sharp edge and prepared surface was probably mounted on a lance and used for attack and defense. A borer with a thin, sharp point was used to punch holes in animal skins for clothes. A gravette point was tied to a spear shaft and thrown. A backed flake, so called because it had a dulled back edge like a pocket knife, probably served as an all-purpose cutting tool. A denticulate tool with a notch may have been the first tool made to make other tools.

BORER

GRAVETTE POINT

BACKED FLAKE

DENTICULATE TOOL

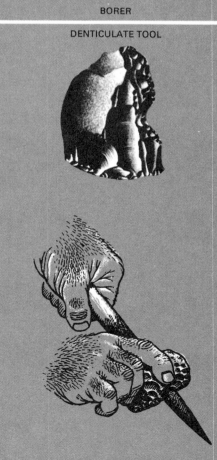

tive Oldowan chopper, which was simply a stone with several chips knocked off one end. The great forward step of the Acheulean core toolmaker was chipping the stone all over. This was a basic improvement that made much more efficient tools. The purpose of the two-sided technique was to flatten the roundish core, for only a flat stone can take a good cutting edge.

The first step in making an Acheulean hand-axe was to shape the core roughly like a turtle shell, thickest in the middle and thinning to a coarse edge all around. The second step was to trim the edge with more delicate flaking. Axes made in this fashion were longer, straighter and much sharper than Oldowan choppers.

Acheulean hand-axes were usually pear-shaped or pointed, and were larger than chopping tools. Some were more than two feet long and weighed more than 25 pounds. Obviously they were too big and heavy for ordinary cutting and scraping; and they may have been set over traps, to fall on the animals that triggered them off.

Another new tool of this period is the cleaver. A cleaver had a straight cutting edge at one end and looked more like a modern ax-head than ancient hand-axes did. It was probably used for heavy chopping.

As Acheulean man developed his craft, he learned to use different kinds of hammers. At first he knocked flakes from a stone core with another stone, leaving irregular scars and wavy cutting edges. But a wood or bone hammer, being softer, gave him greater control over the flaking. Such a hammer left shallower, cleaner scars on a core, and produced sharper and straighter cutting edges. In time, the use of stone on stone was pretty much restricted to the first rough shaping of a hand-axe, and all the edging was done with wood and bone.

In the late Acheulean period a revolutionary toolmaking technique was developed. This was the prepared core—a stone so well chosen and chipped that every flake struck off it was a finished tool. The men who made it had taken a big mental step forward. Chipping a stone into the shape you know you need is one thing, but it is quite another to prepare a core that does not even look like a tool, just so that you can strike finished tools from it.

With all this advanced toolmaking, it is probable that people were also advancing. But here is another rather blank page in the history of early man. The Acheulean industry, introduced by *Homo erectus*, continued until about 60,000 years ago. But the last evidence of *Homo erectus* is at least 250,000 years old, and an entirely different type of man eventually appears and develops a major new tool industry from the Acheulean— Neanderthal man.

Actually the period between *Homo erectus* and Neanderthal man contains a few bits of evidence. The first is a scattering of teeth and jaw fragments discovered in Morocco and France, some of which were found to-

Trying Out Stone Age Tools

To find out what different Paleolithic tools were used for, an imaginative specialist named J. Desmond Clark made copies of them. With the help of Bushmen, he tried them out on different jobs. He then studied the patterns of wear that resulted from different uses and compared them with the patterns on the real tools. He also gave real Stone Age tools to the men, who found that they were remarkably efficient. At right, two Bushmen skin an antelope easily with a stone cleaver; below, another experimenter uses a stone axe to cut a piece of wood from a tree.

gether with Acheulean tools. The teeth look like those of *Homo erectus*.

It is tempting to say, "Well, we know that *Homo erectus* came before this; if teeth like his persist, why not assume that he persisted too?" This would make sense except that other evidence in the form of three skulls from this period seems to contradict this idea. One skull is from Swanscombe, England, one is from Steinheim, Germany, and the third is from Tautavel, France.

The Swanscombe skull turned up near London. It dates from between 200,000 and 300,000 years ago. Although it consists only of three bones from the roof and the back of the head, their size, their proportions and particularly their curves are much the same as modern man's; they are definitely not those of *Homo erectus*. The Swanscombe skull seems to indicate a kind of precocious modern man sneaking into the picture along with, maybe even before, Neanderthal man.

A solution to the puzzle is suggested if we turn to the other skulls, those of Steinheim man in Germany and Tautavel man in France. They, too, have been dated and their age appears to be about the same as Swanscombe man's. While the back of the Tautavel skull is missing, Steinheim man's is not, and it resembles Swanscombe man's. What the skulls from Steinheim and Tautavel add are faces, for the fronts of the skulls have been preserved. And they are not

modern. They have heavy brow ridges and low foreheads that are not quite primitive enough to fall within the range of variation of *Homo erectus* or advanced enough to fall within the range of variation of modern *Homo sapiens*. Clearly they are an intermediate type, and they imply that evolution was working more swiftly on the back of man's head than on his face.

The evidence from Swanscombe man and these skulls is thin, but as pieces are added to

83

the puzzle, it all begins to hang together better and better. For one thing, Acheulean tools have been found at Swanscombe and Tautavel. Once again, the evidence of stone tools adds greatly to the picture.

More tool and fossil evidence will certainly turn up to clarify this period, for the cultural evidence already found is rich and varied. Subcultures arose during the long span of the Acheulean. They are usually named after a peculiar local way of toolmaking. Man's culture was moving in many directions, and as these different threads met and crossed, the fabric of human society grew increasingly widespread and complex. Acheulean tools are found in Europe, Africa, the Middle East and India.

The more developed a culture is, the faster it can respond to local conditions. The skilled toolmakers of the mid-Acheulean period could live virtually anywhere—on the seashore, in the forest or the subtropical savanna. Whatever specialized tools they required in order to succeed in these places, they made themselves.

The tool kit of Neanderthal man, from 100,000 to 40,000 years ago, grows steadily larger, until there are dozens of different styles of axes, borers, choppers, scrapers, knives, notched blades, chisels, planes—not to mention the increasing evidence of antler and bone weapons and tools. It is almost certain that man used wood and bone from the very beginning, but they are much less durable than stone, and almost all the fragments we have go back only to the last days of the Neanderthal period. Among the few exceptions are bits of wood from Torralba in Spain, some 400,000 years old, and a wooden spear from Germany, presumably Neanderthal, that was stuck right through the ribs of a straight-tusked elephant. The first worked bone or ivory also appears at this time, although both are plentiful in the Cro-Magnon period.

The Cro-Magnon culture lasted from 40,000 to 10,000 years ago. Then another new technique appeared: stone tools were ground instead of flaked. With this innovation the Old Stone Age—the Paleolithic—came to an end. Over the course of its two-million-year span man had risen from a state almost like an ape's to a remarkable level of intelligence and achievement.

A Fine Array of Tools

Flint, bone, and antler—three common materials—were used to make these elegantly pointed Stone Age tools. At the top are three hand-axes; below them are delicate flint implements of a later age. At the bottom are some specialized tools of the late Stone Age: needles, harpoon heads and awls.

6

From Neanderthal through Cro-Magnon

For most of us Neanderthal man *is* Stone Age man, the squat, skin-clad beetle-browed fellow we see in the cartoons. We picture him at the mouth of a cave—stone axe in hand, several mammoth bones scattered around—staring out over a snowy landscape as he thinks about the problems of the ice age and the giant cave bear.

There is some truth in this picture. Neanderthals were more primitive than we are (in some ways). They did live in cold climates (sometimes). They probably wore skins (often) and they lived in caves (much of the time). The first fossil skull positively identified as belonging to an ancient man was that of a Neanderthal. Having nothing to compare it with except skulls of modern men, scientists of the time were struck more by the differences between the two than by their similarities. Today the reverse is true.

A GHOSTLY SKULL found in Shanidar Cave in northern Iraq belonged to a 40-year-old Neanderthal man who suffered from arthritis and had a withered arm. This was one of many finds in the Middle East, Africa and Asia that proved Neanderthal man had been widespread.

Put a Neanderthal in a business suit and send him to the supermarket and he might pass completely unnoticed. He might be a little shorter than the man at the checkout counter, but he would not necessarily be the shortest man in the place. He might be heavier-featured, squatter and more muscular than most men, but perhaps not more than the truck driver unloading beer kegs.

In other words, Neanderthal man and modern man overlap. Indeed, the more we learn about the Neanderthals, the more overlapping there appears to be. In fact, Neanderthals are now considered to be members of our own species, *Homo sapiens.* This does not mean that there are not differences between the two. There are plenty.

The first Neanderthal finds came from western Europe, and until the 1930s most of the field work was done in Europe. As discovery followed discovery, it became clear that toward the end of a warm, interglacial period, about 75,000 years ago, Neanderthal peoples were well established in Europe. Moreover, they were always found with a new kind of tool called Mousterian. Wherever these tools are found, we can assume that Neanderthals lived. And Neanderthals are probably descended from people like Swanscombe man and Steinheim man.

This western European Neanderthal, now called the "classic" variety, is not hard to recognize. His skull could hold a brain just as large as modern man's, but it is shaped differently. It has a lower, flatter crown, is

A Wandering Band of Hunters

In the spring, small groups of Neanderthal people like the one shown here set off to look for fresh hunting grounds. They took all their possessions with them—hides and weapons like the stone-tipped spear held by the man at the left. Behind him another man carries skins that can serve as blankets or tent coverings. Women and children are protected in the center of the procession.

longer and bulges more at the back and sides. The face has a massive jaw with a receding chin, broad cheeks and ridges over the eyes that connect across the bridge of the nose. This ridge of bone gives the classic Neanderthal his beetle-browed look.

The rest of the skeleton shows a short, powerfully built man who was just about five and a half feet tall. His arms and legs had short, heavy, slightly curved bones, so he probably looked bowlegged. His hands and feet were also short and stubby.

When the interglacial period ended and the ice spread down over northern Europe once again, Neanderthal peoples still hung on there. On the evidence they left behind, they managed very well. Neanderthal man lived right up to about 35,000 to 40,000 years ago, and then he mysteriously disappeared. His evolution during this period is very puzzling; he seems to have gotten more "primitive," not less so. The last fossils we have from western Europe are even more squat and more beetle-browed than earlier ones.

However, the classic variety is not the only Neanderthal; others, with more modern characteristics, lived along the Mediterranean, in eastern Europe, Asia Minor, Africa, the U.S.S.R., eastern Asia—and just possibly in the Western Hemisphere. The first Neanderthal with modern traits was found in Palestine in 1931. Within the next 30 years more finds in the Middle East showed that some Neanderthals had evolved until, perhaps 40,000 years ago, they were more like Cro-Magnon man than the classic Neanderthal type. But there was great variation, and even here some Neanderthals were almost as classic as their Western cousins.

The Mousterian tools that Neanderthal man developed first appeared toward the end of the interglacial period, when the climate was still mild. He had many kinds of stone tools, bone points and sharpened animal ribs, and he used both core and flake techniques in toolmaking.

His prey varied from mice to mammoths. He ate horse and deer, and as it gradually grew colder he moved into caves and began eating reindeer as his major food source.

Neanderthal man used fire regularly. He probably knew how to start a fire, and he dug hearths in the floors of his caves. He was a home builder as well as a cave dweller. One of several sites in Russia where he lived is marked by a ring of hearths; outside that is a circle of heavy elephant bones and tusks that may have formed a framework for a skin tent. Neanderthals undoubtedly also made temporary shelters of sticks and grass.

Neanderthal man apparently stood on the edge of becoming an artist. For the first time in human experience, faint signs of decoration appear; he began scratching designs on bones. But his most important cultural accomplishment was that he felt the first stirrings of a social and religious sense. For one thing, he buried his dead. This suggests that he realized life was fleeting, that he was concerned about the future, and that he may also have cared for the older members of his

The Cult of the Cave Bear

The ferocious cave bear, a massive animal that stood eight feet tall when it reared up in anger, must have been extremely dangerous to hunt. Yet there is much evidence that Neanderthal man did hunt it often. Perhaps the animal's fierceness made the hunt a kind of ritual—the men may have hunted the bear for trophies. This possibility is suggested by the strange arrangement of bear bones above.

group. A number of Neanderthal burial sites have been found, both in western and eastern Europe, and they reveal a good deal. The most impressive burial was discovered at Shanidar Cave in northern Iraq. At the rear of the cave was a 60,000-year-old grave of a hunter whose skull had been badly crushed. Examination of the soil in and around the grave revealed that flowers had been placed with the body. Other Neanderthal burial sites show thoughtful additions of tools and bones. Clearly, Neanderthal man believed in some kind of life after death.

About 40,000 years ago people practically identical to those of today appeared. They appeared gradually, and they were not all alike, any more than they are now. But the date of 35,000 B.C. marks the establishment of *Homo sapiens*—after that, earlier forms of man are no longer seen.

As usual, the evidence is lopsided and incomplete, mainly because most of the work that deals with the period 40,000 to 10,000 years ago is concentrated in Europe. So we know quite a bit about the people who lived there during those years, but much less about those who lived in other places. We

The Unending Search for Food

Neanderthals were clever hunters and had many ways of getting food. At left, they chase mountain sheep across a chasm; the strong ones will jump the gap, the weak ones will fall down and be killed. At right, hunters return to their cave with a graylag goose and an ibex. Neanderthals sometimes ate human flesh too, as shown above.

know that there were people in Africa and Asia, and that men first invaded Australia and North America, and later South America. But these areas were not investigated in detail, as were those in Europe, particularly in France in the region of the Dordogne.

The Dordogne is laced with rivers that empty into the Atlantic at Bordeaux. Long ago the rivers scoured out a series of narrow valleys with steep rock walls rising 200 or 300 feet. This is a world of limestone, pockmarked with caves, grottoes and overhangs. Neanderthals began appearing in these sheltered places at the beginning of the last ice age, and men have lived there ever since. In a way they are still inhabited, for many a modern house is tucked under a bulging overhang of rock that forms its back wall.

The possibility that early man lived in the Dordogne was first explored a century ago by a lawyer turned anthropologist, Edouard Lartet. He began to inspect caves at Les Eyzies and other spots in the Vézère River Valley. Traces of man were everywhere. As discovery followed discovery, it became clear that the area had been populated for thousands of years. Today there are hundreds of known sites of prehistoric human occupation in the Dordogne.

The great cave at Lascaux, the most dramatic yet found, was discovered in 1940 when a dog fell into a hole left by an uprooted tree. The boys with the dog widened the crack and slipped down into a cavern hundreds of feet long. Here they found the rock walls covered with paintings of horses, deer and bison. In 1868 workers widening a highway at Les Eyzies cut into a roadside rock shelter known as "Cro-Magnon" (in the local dialect, "big hole"). They uncovered some carefully buried skeletons and stone tools. This place gave its name to the people who lived not only in France but in many parts of Europe at the end of the last ice age. They were a little shorter than their modern relatives and had slightly larger heads. They had prominent chins and high-bridged noses, small, even teeth and broad, strong faces. Their brain capacity was just as large as the average for modern Europeans.

With this large brain, Cro-Magnon man produced a culture far more advanced than Neanderthal man's. He inherited many of the tool techniques of Neanderthal man, but he developed some fine, new ones for working stone and particularly bone. Even more impressive was his fantastic artistic ability. There are dozens of sites of Cro-Magnon cave art in France alone, dating from about 28,000 to 10,000 B.C. Cro-Magnon man was a close observer of the animals he hunted, and a magnificent artist. More than that, he was able to appreciate and encourage these talents and to work them into his dreams and rituals. His artistic work apparently tied in closely with his spiritual life.

One strong indication of this is seen in the places he chose to put his wall paintings. There are basically two kinds of caves in the Dordogne. First there are the rock over-

A House Built with Bones

The dome-shaped hut shown here may have been one kind of home that Stone Age man lived in. Archeologists think so because they discovered a site, shown in the diagram at right, where a group of mammoth bones were lying in a semicircle, suggesting that they had been a part of some round structure. Probably the original hut was draped with animal hides held down by other bones. Some of the bones were found to have holes in them and may have been used as mounts for poles *(top picture)* that supported the structure.

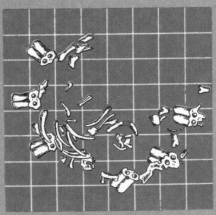

Cro-Magnon, a Modern Man

Some 40,000 years ago Neanderthal man was replaced in Europe by a robust, tall and intelligent kind of man called Cro-Magnon (*below*). He had a well-developed culture which included elaborate burial ceremonies like the one shown at right. In this scene tribe members bury a hunter, placing a tusk in his grave and sprinkling him with a red dirt to make him look more lifelike. Two other hunters wait to cover his body with a huge mammoth's bone.

hangs, more or less open and facing out over the valleys, which can be made more livable by putting up barriers of brushwood or of animal skins to keep out the cold winds of winter. These are the ones that Cro-Magnon man lived in, leaving evidence of his tools and fireplaces at many levels.

There are some fragments of decoration in these open cave homes. But the spectacular Cro-Magnon wall art is in the Dordogne's true caves: deep underground fissures with long galleries and passages that have subterranean pools and rivers, and festoons of stalactites hanging from the ceilings. Such caves are dark and mysterious; to see inside them lamps or torches are needed. The caves apparently were used for ritual ceremonies, or as shrines, since they contain little or no evidence of habitation.

It is also worth noting that paintings and sculptures were frequently made in the worst possible places—in narrow niches, behind

bumps of rock, sometimes in areas where it must have been not only difficult but even dangerous for the artist to work. This art could not have been meant to be admired.

What was its purpose then? According to experts, much of the art was an attempt at magic—hunting magic. Cro-Magnon man was a hunter. He was strong and intelligent; and equipped with all kinds of weapons, from spears and knives to slings. He made traps for small animals and pitfalls for large ones. He could ambush and stampede. He has left impressive records of his skill. In Předmost, Czechoslovakia, there are skeletons of 100 mammoths, and below the great cliff at Solutré lie the remains of more than 10,000 horses. But Cro-Magnon man also knew he had to deal with forces beyond his control, including unfriendly ones. Bad luck might mean death, for some of his prey was extremely dangerous. The hunter had to

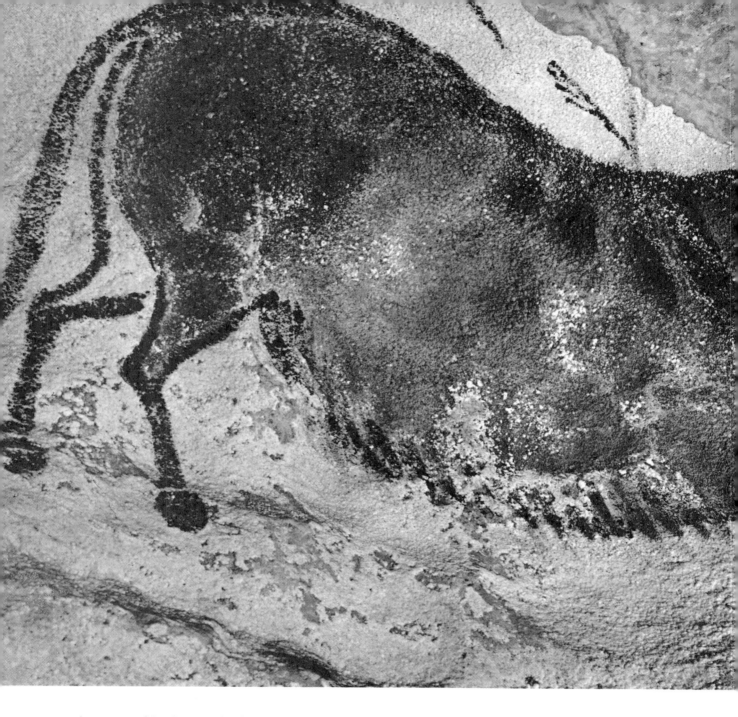

have good luck, too; he had to be able to find and kill an animal. He improved his chances by painting a picture of the animal that he hoped to kill and then performing religious or magical rites in order to strengthen the power of his wish picture.

This is not all guesswork; a variety of evidence supports it. First, there are the many animals painted with spears stuck in them, or marked with the blows of clubs—clearly to show what the hunters fervently hoped would happen in the actual hunt. In a cave near Les Eyzies, there are several drawings of trapped animals, including a picture of a

Magical Cave Paintings

One of the most remarkable things about Cro-Magnon man is that he decorated many caves, like the one below, with accurate and beautiful pictures of animals. These pictures were probably supposed to work magic, for they were mostly of animals, like the horse (*left*), which Cro-Magnon man hunted. Probably they believed that painting an animal would make it easier to catch.

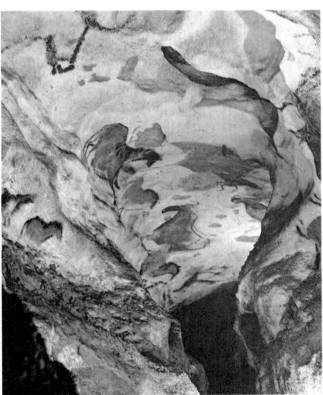

mammoth in a pit. Another clue to the nature of the art is the fact that many new heads are painted over earlier pictures. In one spot at Lascaux there are four layers of heads, suggesting that each new picture was made for new magic—for a future hunt of a different animal. The concentration of paintings at certain spots suggests that these spots were considered especially lucky, particularly since there are empty wall spaces nearby. Favorite wall space must have been where previous paintings had worked good magic. At Les Combarelles there are nearly 300 animals engraved on the rocks. Crowd-

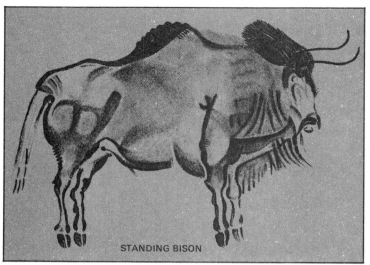

STANDING BISON

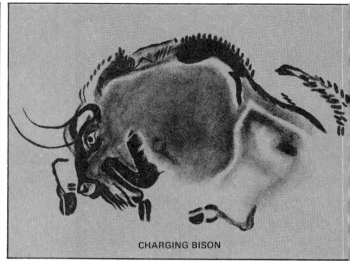

CHARGING BISON

ing of this kind may be why Cro-Magnon artists often painted one animal's head on another's body. Or perhaps the artist saved time in representing new quarry by making the body of the old one do. We can imagine a man looking at a large, handsome picture of a bison, and deciding it would be enough just to paint a deer's head over the bison's.

Hunting magic could also explain the occasional man-beast figures that are found in some caves—strange-looking creatures with human bodies and animal or bird heads, often looking as though they are dancing. These figures may be pictures of hunters dressed up as animals and may have been made to guarantee a successful hunt. On the other hand, they may be symbols. Perhaps a hunter felt that a painting of a magician doing a ritual dance would work magic on the animals he was going to hunt. Or the man-beast figures may have indicated a super-human being, such as a spirit of the hunt.

Although the Cro-Magnon paintings are stunning, they cover a very limited number of subjects. There are few full scenes and, besides the sorcerers, almost no people. This is natural, for anyone who thinks that pictures are dangerous magic would not be likely to draw a picture of himself. Late Stone Age man painted mainly mammals, and of these, only about a dozen of the commonest big game mammals. Very occasionally something like a bird, a fish or a snake was drawn. The animals are always shown in profile with sure, bold outlines. The artists used different colored earths and clays, mixed with charcoal and animal fat. They applied the color either by using a crude crayon made of this mixture or by blowing dry powdered colors onto the wall through a hollow bone. The colors were slowly absorbed by the limestone walls, which explains why they have lasted so long. Much of Cro-Magnon art has retained its original brilliance for 10,000 or

HUNTING GOD OR MEDICINE MAN

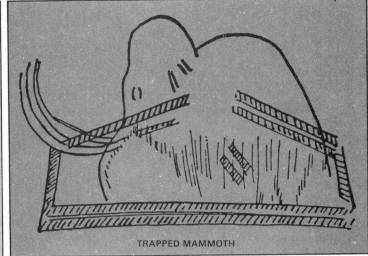

TRAPPED MAMMOTH

Art to Help the Hunt

The magnificent paintings and engravings of animals that Stone Age man decorated his caves with were probably intended to help him in the hunt. Many showed trapped or dying animals, like the mammoth in the trap above, and the bear below covered with spear marks. Others show creatures like the one at left, which seem to be part animal and part man. This one may have been a hunting god, or a tribal medicine man dressed in skins for a hunting ceremony.

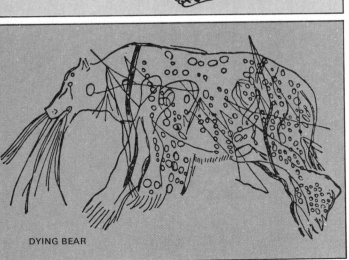

DYING BEAR

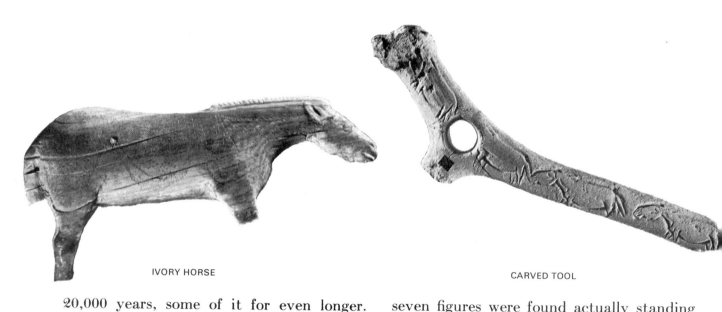

IVORY HORSE   CARVED TOOL

20,000 years, some of it for even longer.

Cro-Magnon man was not only a good painter, but a fairly good sculptor and engraver too. He chiseled animal outlines on cave walls and went on to sculpt in high relief. Le Cap Blanc, near Les Eyzies, has a marvelous set of horses, carved so that the natural curves of the rock emphasize their rounded bodies. Cro-Magnon man also made statues in the round. These statuettes, all of women, are found all over Europe and as far east as Siberia. They look like tiny earth goddesses or mother figures and the best opinions suggest that they were.

Most of these statuettes come from the period between 20,000 and 25,000 years ago when the weather ranged from cool to very cold. Though the cold periods were bitter, especially on the eastern European plains, many people still lived there. Their homes were shallow pits in the ground roofed with hides or sod. The outlines of many of these huts may still be seen. Many female figurines were found in such sites, often lying beside the walls. At one site in the Ukraine

seven figures were found actually standing on the walls. The statuettes often taper to a point at the bottom as if they were made to be stuck in a base. It is fairly clear that the figurines were close to the homes and daily lives of the peoples who made them, and have a quite different purpose from the wall art in secret underground caves. But whether they were merely household good-luck charms or mother goddesses, nobody knows. They whisper to us about the lives of their creators, but say nothing about themselves.

Death, as well as life, concerned Cro-Magnon man, and his treatment of his dead was thoughtful. He dug graves down into the underlying layers of ashes left from previous occupations of a living site, and protected the bodies by covering them with stones. He also sprinkled red ocher on the dead to make their pale skins look healthy.

The Neanderthal practice of including objects in graves with the dead led, in Cro-Magnon times, to elaborate burials. In a Stone Age settlement found approximately 130 miles northeast of Moscow, the grave of

STYLIZED MAMMOTH

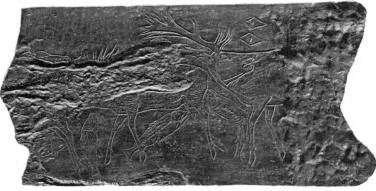

REINDEER AND SALMON FIGURES

two young boys suggests either that the boys were very important or that the people who lived there 23,000 years ago were much concerned with an afterlife. The boys were laid out in a line, head to head. Both had been dressed from head to toe in clothing decorated with ivory beads carved from mammoth tusks, and they wore bracelets and rings of the same material. On one boy's chest lay a disk of mammoth tusk carved into the shape of a horse. Both boys had an assortment of ivory weapons such as lances, spears and daggers. The lances had been formed from a split mammoth bone that had been warmed over a fire in order to straighten it—quite a difficult thing to do.

Not all the human skeletons from the late Stone Age show such ritual. Large numbers of human bones are scattered helter-skelter. Some leg bones have been cracked apart, as if someone had wanted the marrow in them; sometimes, skulls have been smashed open from behind, perhaps to reach the brains. This raises the horror of cannibalism, which apparently had been practiced even in the

A Great Variety of Art

Besides making magnificent cave paintings, Paleolithic people also made delicate carvings and engravings. Most of these were of animals, like the ones shown at the tops of these two pages. At far left is a lifelike horse, and a tool covered with engraved horses. Directly above is an antler carved with reindeer and salmon; to its left is a stylized mammoth. The artists rarely depicted men, but they did make sculptures of women, like the one below, which may have been meant to be worshiped.

IVORY WOMAN'S HEAD

103

days of Peking man. Whatever use was made of human bones seems to have been largely associated with rituals.

Many of today's primitive societies keep skulls, and even civilized people keep the ashes of their ancestors in urns. There are intriguing bits of evidence that Cro-Magnon man was a skull-and-bone man. One cave in France held three human skulls that had purposely been placed on a slab of rock. Another cave contained the skull of a woman with a number of shell ornaments arranged around it. Elsewhere in this same cave were pieces of skulls arranged with equal care. Close examination suggests these pieces were used as shallow cups. To begin with, they were arranged in a row and lying open side up. Each one bore marks on its surface indicating that the muscles and flesh that originally covered it had been hacked or scraped away with some kind of stone tool and that the lower parts of the skull had then been chopped off and the rough edges smoothed all around, leaving a skull cap that actually made a shallow cup.

Aside from the way Cro-Magnon handled his skeletal remains, he also left clues to his everyday life and how he coped with the world around him. Excavations in the Middle East, in South Africa, in Japan and Siberia, in Southeast Asia, and in North and Central America all suggest that the last humans to use stone and bone exclusively for their weapons and tools were people of many and varied achievements. Able to adapt to changes in their environment, some migrated to the very northernmost parts of Siberia. Others got to Australia from Southeast Asia. They could only have done so by boat. What sort of boat it was we do not know. But we do know that the Java Trench across which they sailed was 60 miles wide during the late Stone Age—and 26,000 feet deep. Whatever its shape and size, the boat had to be seaworthy with some sort of steering device.

The more we learn about Cro-Magnon, the narrower the gap will become between that form of modern man and ourselves. Unfortunately, the intimate details of social life, the games children played, the little things that give a society its quality—all these have vanished like smoke. We have no knowledge of how one Cro-Magnon spoke to another. And we never will know.

A Specialist in Cave Art

Much of what we know today about Stone Age art comes from a French priest, the Abbé Henri Breuil. He devoted his life to studying the art and spent long hours crawling in cold, clammy underground passages (*right*). He was among the first people to believe that these paintings were from the Stone Age.

AUSTRALIAN ABORIGINES are a primitive people whose life is similar in some ways to early man's. Here a group of men, painted with special markings for the occasion, are doing a dance symbolic of a hunt. One hops around imitating a kangaroo, while another pretends to throw a spear at him.

7

How the Savage
Lives On in Man

It may seem startling that *Homo habilis*,
Homo erectus, Neanderthal man and all the
others have anything to teach us today.
But that is precisely the point of the new
paleoanthropology, which seeks not simply
museum collections of old bones but also specific relationships between modern men and
their ancestors.

We study ancient man not just out of curiosity, but also to learn about ourselves.
There is much about modern man—about

his society, about his deepest beliefs, about his sudden lapses into savagery—that is not well understood. We can learn more about such matters if we understand their origins better. To do that we must become more familiar with our ancestors and recognize that the gap separating us from at least our immediate ancestors is more in the culture we have developed than in any inborn ability. Peoples living 10,000 or 20,000 years ago probably would do as well with our tools as we are doing today. And if we were put back there—with no metals, no agriculture, no domestic animals, no written language, and most important, no idea that these things were possible—we would probably do no better than they did. We forget that early man did not have these four principal assets on which modern society is based.

In studying ancient man we are really studying simplified versions of ourselves. This is why modern paleoanthropologists are

ADULT LIFE

DEATH

The Life of a Hunter

so interested in exploring everything at a given digging site to learn more about how early man lived. We find clues, but we have very little exact knowledge. We know for example that Cro-Magnon people made needles with eyes in them, and we can guess from this that they stitched animal skins together to make clothing. But we have no idea whether men or women made the clothing, and this would be important information. Do the bone needles and other delicate tools

An aborigine's life is spent mostly in hunting and food gathering. This painting, done in the style of aborigine art, shows activities from birth to death. At far left, an expectant mother gathers wild yams, while two young children hunt lizards and birds. After being initiated into manhood (*box*) an adult goes on to hunt bigger and stronger animals such as kangaroos. At far right, an old man dies; aborigines believe that his soul will be reborn.

reflect a woman's tool kit, or were there men who specialized in tailoring? In short, did early man divide up work into special jobs?

We are inclined to believe that as far back as *Homo erectus* there was some such division among men and women and even among men and other men. Such aspects of early behavior could shed light on patterns in later human societies: division of labor by sex, a male work force divided into specialties, what was considered menial versus dignified occupations.

These patterns of behavior are what paleoanthropologists try to reconstruct. Take the idea of food sharing. Except for chimpanzees, man is the only primate who makes a practice of sharing his food with his fellows. How, where and why did he get this idea? Cro-Magnon man obviously did, so did Neanderthal man, and so, apparently, did *Homo erectus*. All of them had more or less permanent home bases to which the hunters brought back food. So, perhaps, did *Homo habilis*, for animal fossils are also found in his sites. The practice developed early and is obviously very important to human evolution, since close family ties, child care and teaching are all basic requirements of human society. But we do not know when it started.

Nor do we know when the idea of permanent mates arose. Study of primates in the wild, which is increasingly used to help interpret the past, reveals that few, even among the higher apes, have long-term male-female relationships. Most mating partners are tak-

en only for short periods of time. Yet men and women today marry and form lifelong pairs, and they presumably have done so for thousands of years. But we cannot be sure. We know nothing of the family customs of Cro-Magnon man, let alone of his predecessors. All we know is that modern man is sexually possessive. This trait is so deep-seated that it clearly goes a long way back.

What the most primitive modern societies do have in common with each other and with paleolithic societies is that they all live by hunting and gathering, and not by agriculture. That kind of existence limits the size of social units, since large numbers of men cannot hunt and gather in a small area and survive. Bands of aborigines seldom exceed 50 individuals and are often limited to a single family. Of course they do mingle with other groups like their own; sometimes they walk many miles to attend large song-and-dance festivals. Their society is loosely organized into larger groups that have clearly defined territories within which each small family band operates. But the basic unit is the family, and it is monogamous—one man to one wife. In a hunter-gatherer society a man cannot support more than one wife.

It is very likely that prehistoric hunting societies also lived in small groups and that they too were basically monogamous. It may be that monogamy began with the gradual development of a home, which in turn may have had its origin in hunting.

A Musical People

African Bushmen were once excellent artists, as many old rock paintings show. Today they have lost much of their interest in painting and decoration, but they take a great delight in music. At left, a Bushman plays a musical bow, an instrument that developed from the hunting bow. He puts one end in his mouth and picks the wire string; the sound is something like two flutes being played at once. Below, a woman plays a thumb piano by pressing and releasing metal prongs, while her companion lights a pipe and listens.

As long as the emphasis was on gathering, a band of hominids probably acted much like a band of apes, moving slowly about, eating what it could find in the way of vegetables, berries, fruits and nuts. There was probably little food-sharing, since all members of the band knew how to gather food from the time they were children. However, as hunting became more important than gathering, getting food became more and more the responsibility of the males. It became more and more dangerous for females and young to tag along, and probably impossible for them to keep up if the hunt was a long, hard one. For females and infants, hunting came to mean waiting in a safe place for the hunters to return with food. Thus food-sharing, homemaking and monogamy probably all grew up more or less together.

All these conclusions are based largely on what we know of modern man, rather than on what has been dug out of the past. As a psychiatrist has said, one of the best relics we have of early man is modern man. Psychologists and psychiatrists are trying to find out more about the problems of stress

A Bushman's Camp

Small grass huts serve as temporary shelters for two families of Bushmen who are out searching for food. While they live here the women gather nuts from trees, collect them in piles on the ground (*left foreground*) and roast them over small fires. While the women and children stay close to camp, the men hunt animals.

and aggression in modern life, and how these forces affect the physical and emotional health of people today. In their search for causes they soon find themselves talking to paleoanthropologists, pooling ideas and information to discover the origins of emotional patterns that perhaps arose thousands of years ago.

How emotional states are associated with bodily changes; why these changes take place and what use they are to man was not clearly understood until this century. In the 1920s a physiologist, Walter Cannon, made a classic study of the hormone adrena-

lin and its effects on the nervous system. He discovered that it acted like a "shot in the arm" releasing carbohydrates stored in the liver and pouring them into the blood stream in the form of sugar for quick energy. He also found that adrenalin increased the flow of blood to the heart, lungs, central nervous system and limbs. These changes help a person fight off fatigue, move more speedily and have greater endurance.

Adrenalin is released during periods of intense emotion, whether or not these periods are followed by activity. All a man has to do is feel a rush of fright or anger and his

Food Gathering Is Women's Business Too

All members of an Australian aborigine tribe help in getting food. In the picture above, a woman fills a straw bag with fruit from a cycad palm tree. Although this fruit is poisonous, it can be soaked and peeled to make it edible. At right, two young girls play with a mangrove crab they have caught. They have learned where to find food in their own area, but when they grow up and marry they will probably move to a different place. Then they will have to learn how to find new kinds of food.

system's emergency reaction will prepare him for what he has to do next. Obviously adrenalin has great survival value in a "fight-or-flight" situation.

This checks very well with studies of hunter-gatherers living today. Irven De Vore and Richard Lee carried out a field study of Bushmen in Africa. They found that Bushmen often face situations that are greatly eased by adrenalin. The excitement of seeing and stalking an animal triggers the response that will be needed to attack and kill it in a sudden surge.

These bursts of exertion are only part of the Bushmen's hunting activity. They often trail an animal for many weary miles before reaching it. Then, tired as they may be, they must still have enough energy to sprint forward and plant a poisoned arrow before the animal runs out of range. If the animal is big, the poison will take effect slowly and the Bushmen may have to follow it doggedly for miles, sometimes for days, before they are able to close in and kill it. During this long chase they may eat only a handful of food from time to time to keep them going as they run. But once their adrenalin has started flowing, their body resources help them keep going. Other materials such as cholesterol and fatty acids also build up in the blood stream, to be worked off during the long tracking.

This discussion of adrenalin may seem to have taken us rather far from the behavior of early man, but that nasty word

cholesterol brings us to the new study of the effects of stress situations on the human body. Modern man, although he no longer lives a hunting life, is still physically a hunter-gatherer. His body is still efficient at facing sudden danger and going hungry for long periods while tracking prey. His glands react just as they have for hundreds of thousands of years. Unfortunately he has no chance to burn off the materials that once aided him; he lives a sedentary life, and while the stresses come one after another, their side effects build up in his system and do him all kinds of harm. Many sci-

entists note that we are physically equipped for one kind of life but live another, and they wonder whether there is any connection between such primitive emotional reactions as aggression and such modern ailments as heart disease.

There could be connections indeed. For instance, doctors think cholesterol plays a part in coronary heart disease. If strong emotions build up dangerous levels of cholesterol in a man and modern life gives him no chance to burn it up, then obviously man is not equipped for modern life. He is

still back in the Stone Age emotionally— and the strain is killing him.

Consider the businessman on his way to an important conference. His success or failure may depend on how aggressively he takes charge of the meeting, beats down the arguments of others, rallies support to his point of view. Although no physical energy will be spent this still promises to be a real battle, and in preparation for it his system has been churning out hormones since he got up that morning. He is aroused by a challenging situation, and even more aroused as other challenges in the meeting

Catching a Springhaas

Two Bushmen work as a team to catch a springhaas, a small animal that lives in a burrow. At far left, one man begins digging while the other holds the animal in its burrow with the metal tip of a long pole. In the middle picture, the digger, furiously scooping dirt, crouches up to his shoulders in the hole. He grabs the kicking animal in triumph (*above*) and takes it home to make a meal of fresh meat.

trigger off still higher levels of cholesterol and fatty acids in his blood. At the end of the morning he sits down to a couple of cocktails and a heavy lunch. Then the meetings continue in the afternoon. If they go badly for him, the tension may continue far into the night.

His glandular system has responded with great efficiency to the demands made on it, but if he cannot burn up the accumulations in his blood stream with vigorous physical activity, then our businessman is in serious trouble. His safety valve is gone. He cannot change the reactions of his glands to his nervous system. The only way out is to change his way of life. So we should learn as much as we can about the ways of hunter-gatherers, if only to find out what our systems were designed for, so that we may perhaps lead healthier lives.

Taking a brisk walk after such a tension-building situation might help a little. Many doctors recommend walking and cycling as exercise for heart patients. Paleoanthropologists know that man has slowly adapted to efficient upright striding and his long life as a hunter-gatherer required a great deal of steady walking. To ignore this way of life, they realize, may be just as dangerous as keeping a large and vigorous hunting dog cooped up in a city apartment or trying to adapt a lowland marsh plant to life on a mountaintop. Neither dog nor flower would do very well in its new environment. The surprising thing about man is that he does as well as he does in the light of his past.

Still, man is changing in response to his new environment; the principles of natural selection still work for him as they always have. If our environment were to stay as it is long enough, probably the aggressive tendencies that we have inherited from our ancestors would finally eliminate themselves by killing off, through heart attacks and other ailments, those of us who still carried those primitive traits. Certainly the world would be a nicer and much safer place to live in if people were gentler and more patient than they are. We might even make a long guess that the high death rate from coronary disease among American men today could be a result of natural selection. It may be weeding out a part of the population that is well adapted to short-term success, but poorly adapted to survival in our society. Given time, the overall ability to survive should win out over the competitive drive to succeed.

The problem is that there is not enough time. Human culture is developing so fast it leaves man flat-footed, tied to the slow process of selection, which takes hundreds of thousands of years to produce significant differences in the human species. As René Dubos of The Rockefeller University has said: "Even when man has become an urbane city dweller, the paleolithic bull which survives in his inner self still paws the earth whenever a threatening gesture is made on the social scene." Given emotionally out-

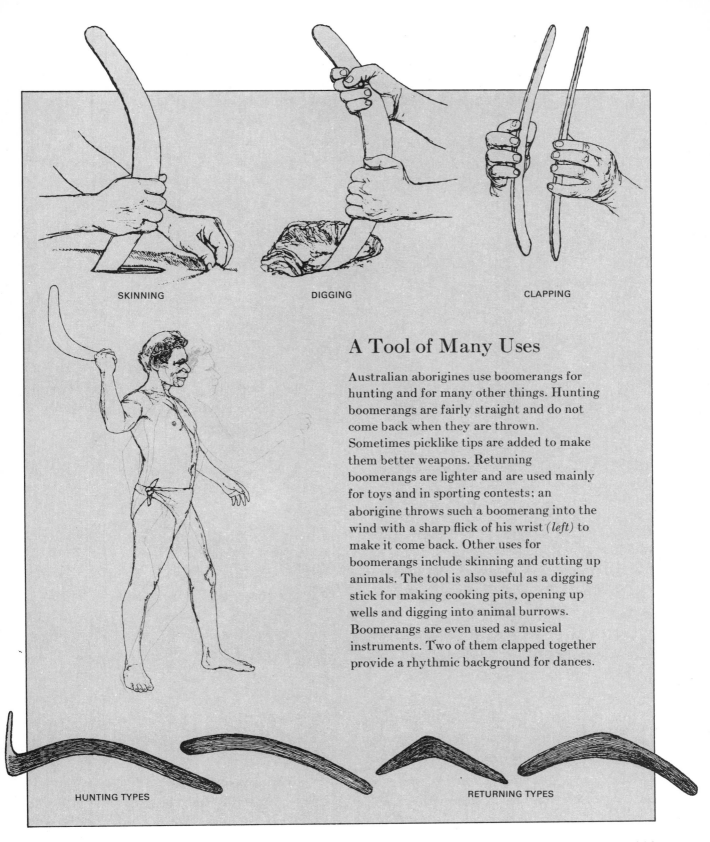

SKINNING

DIGGING

CLAPPING

A Tool of Many Uses

Australian aborigines use boomerangs for hunting and for many other things. Hunting boomerangs are fairly straight and do not come back when they are thrown. Sometimes picklike tips are added to make them better weapons. Returning boomerangs are lighter and are used mainly for toys and in sporting contests; an aborigine throws such a boomerang into the wind with a sharp flick of his wrist (*left*) to make it come back. Other uses for boomerangs include skinning and cutting up animals. The tool is also useful as a digging stick for making cooking pits, opening up wells and digging into animal burrows. Boomerangs are even used as musical instruments. Two of them clapped together provide a rhythmic background for dances.

HUNTING TYPES

RETURNING TYPES

SECRETARY BIRD

Sign Language for Hunting

When Bushmen hunt they chatter with each other until they see an animal or pick up its trail. Then they stalk in silence, using hand signals to keep each other informed. Most of the signals identify different animals by their most noticeable features. Thus the signal for an ostrich mimics the bird's long neck, and the one for a tortoise resembles the shape of its back. The vervet monkey, on the other hand, is indicated simply by the palm of the hand held flat. This means that the monkey is "like a man."

dated men like that and the fearsome power of modern weapons, the primitive emotions could win out over culture simply by blowing culture off the face of the earth. Then, if we should find ourselves scampering around after our food again, at least we would be doing what our bodies were designed for. We are not doing it now.

All of this may seem to suggest that there is something damaging about culture —if all it can do is produce more heart attacks and worse wars. Nothing could be further from the truth. Success in nature is measured by what happens to the species as a whole, not by what happens to its individual members. And as a species man has been overwhelmingly successful—as his sheer numbers prove. It has been estimated that two million years ago the hominid population of the earth was not much over 100,000 individuals, probably all of them australopithecines living in Africa. Three hundred thousand years ago, toward the end

of *Homo erectus*' known span, the human population was probably one million, and by 25,000 years ago, during the Cro-Magnon period, it had jumped to more than three million. Since then it has risen at an increasingly rapid pace. An idea of this increasing speed is brought home by the fact that about 3 per cent of all the human beings who have ever lived are alive right now. People are also living longer. While Neanderthals had a life expectancy of about 29 years, people in advanced societies today can expect to live about 70 years.

The population of the world has not increased steadily but in a series of surges, reflecting man's great cultural steps. The first step, of course, was the development of stone tools. This allowed for a population increase in two ways: tools made it possible to live in many places where people without tools could not survive; with tools people were more efficient and could make better use of their environment. In the days of crude chopping tools some two million years

BIRDS

HAWK

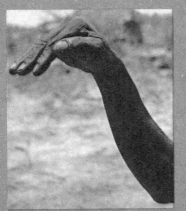

OSTRICH

CROWNED GUINEA FOWL

DUCK

SMALL ANIMALS

RATEL

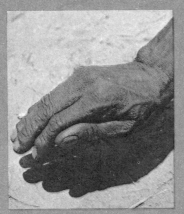

SMALL TORTOISE

PORCUPINE

VERVET MONKEY

LARGER ANIMALS

HARTEBEEST

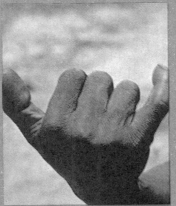

GNU

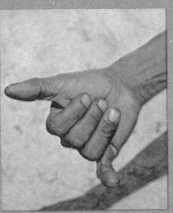

WART HOG

LION

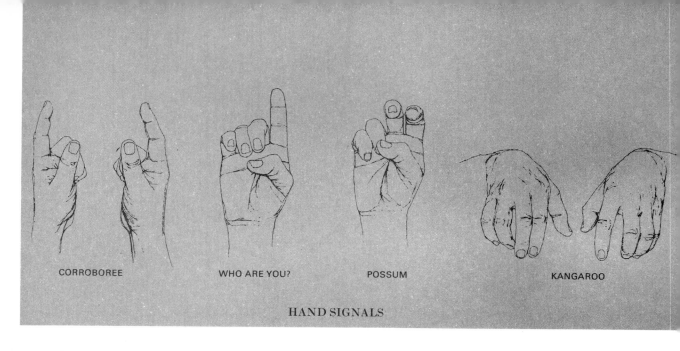

CORROBOREE WHO ARE YOU? POSSUM KANGAROO

HAND SIGNALS

ago, the population density of Africa has been estimated at only one individual per 100 square miles. By the end of the Paleolithic, or Old Stone Age, when men had learned how to grind tools to obtain the shapes they desired, their density had risen to one for every 10 square miles.

The second step that speeded population growth was the double discovery of how to grow crops and how to domesticate animals. This came about 10,000 years ago. It enabled people to settle down permanently and to live together in large numbers for the first time. Even nomadic herdsmen could exist in far greater concentrations on a given area of land than hunters could. The effect on world population was staggering. In 4,000 years it jumped from an estimated five million to 86 million.

The third step was the industrial age that began approximately 300 years ago. The population at that time was some 550 million; today the population has increased to some four billion.

While these figures are impressive, they are not as impressive as the general speed-up that has been taking place. It took two million years to get through the Old Stone Age. The second step took only 10,000 years, and the third has been going on for only a few hundred. How long it will continue or what the population of the earth will finally be is anybody's guess. But since there is only so much room on the earth, we should reach the limit pretty soon.

It is impossible to predict how man will handle this problem. It is all very well to talk about the success of the species as a whole, but if this can only be accomplished at the expense of uncontrolled crowding and almost world-wide misery, then there is something wrong. Man is not just another species of animal. He is the first animal in the history of the world who at last understands something of his place in it and the laws that govern his own activities. He is unique in having within his grasp the possibility of solving the dreadful dilemma of

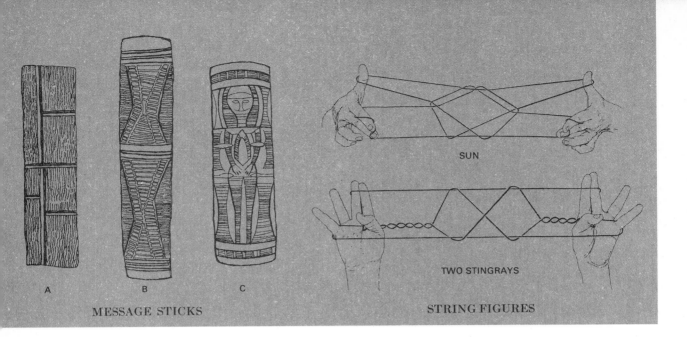

A   B   C

MESSAGE STICKS   STRING FIGURES

SUN

TWO STINGRAYS

his numbers. But the mere fact that he can is no guarantee that he will. Every day the front pages of the newspapers scream out the evidence that even now man acts, emotionally, like a savage.

For all his culture, the one thing of value that modern man has achieved is a good deal of knowledge and understanding of himself and the world. Much of this knowledge is not yet available to large numbers of men; sadly, it is rejected by many others. Nevertheless it is there. The principles of evolution described in this book are true, and we ignore them at our own risk. They have a vital bearing on man's understanding of himself and thus they affect the future of us all, since it is only a matter of time before we will have it in our power to direct our own evolution. Here—and not in space shots—lies man's greatest challenge. For the first time in the 3.5-billion-year history of life there will be a chance to combine the good of the species with the good of the individual.

Communicating without Words

Australian aborigines must keep quiet during hunts and certain ceremonies, and they have developed ways of communicating without making any noise. Hand signals (*far left*) are used to identify animals and to ask questions; similar signals are used by old women, who find them easier than talking. Carved message sticks are employed for making lists (*A*), "IOUs" (*B*) and invitations (*C*). String figures are used for telling stories and in ceremonies; the aborigines have over 400 different patterns.

DANCING IN THE DAWN, two African Bushmen raise clouds of fine dust, while other tribesmen sit and watch.

The ancient ritual of dancing survives in modern life as a reminder of our primitive heritage from early man.

Index

Numerals in italics indicate a photograph
or painting of the subject listed.

Credits

The sources for the illustrations that appear in this book are shown below. Credits for the pictures from left to right are separated by commas, from top to bottom by dashes.

For Further Reading

Avi-Yonah, Michael, *Digging Up the Past.* Lerner Publications, 1974.
Baldwin, Gordon C., *Stone Age Peoples Today.* W. W. Norton, 1964.
Bauman, Hans, *The Caves of the Great Hunters.* Pantheon Books, 1962.
Cohen, Daniel, *Secrets from Ancient Graves.* Dodd, Mead, 1968.
Day, Michael H., *Fossil Man.* Bantam Books, 1971.
DeCamp, L. S., *Darwin and His Great Discovery.* Macmillan, 1972.
Freed, Stanley A. and Ruth S., *Man from the Beginning.* Creative Education, 1967.

Frimmer, Steven, *Finding the Forgotten.* G. P. Putnam's Sons, 1971.
Goode, Ruth, *People of the Ice Age.* Macmillan, 1973.
Greis, Noel P., *Early Man.* Pendulum Press, 1975.
Halacy, D. S., Jr., *Social Man: The Relationships of Humankind.* Macrae, 1973.
Hays, H. R., *Explorers of Man.* Macmillan, 1971.
Janus, Christopher G., and William Brashler, *The Search for Peking Man.* Macmillan, 1975.
Lerner, Marguerite R., *Where Do You Come From: The Story of Evolution.* Lerner Publications, 1967.

McBride, Angus, *The Way They Lived.* Soccer, 1976.
Mead, Margaret:
Anthropologists and What They Do. Franklin Watts, 1965.
People and Places. Collins World, 1959.
Munck, Eckehard, *Biology of the Future.* Franklin Watts, 1974.
Pfeiffer, John E., and Carleton S. Coon, *The Search for Early Man.* American Heritage, 1963.
Ronen, Avraham, *Introducing Prehistory: Digging Into the Past.* Lerner Publications, 1976.
Silverberg, Robert:

Clocks for the Ages: How Scientists Date the Past. Macmillan, 1971.
Morning of Mankind: Prehistoric Man in Europe. New York Graphic Society, 1967.
Stilwell, Hart, *Looking at Man's Past.* Steck-Vaughn, 1965.
Stoutenburg, Adrien, *People in Twilight: Vanishing and Changing Cultures.* Doubleday, 1971.
Suggs, Robert C., *Modern Discoveries in Archeology.* Crowell, 1962.
White, Anne Terry, and Gerald S. Lietz, *Built to Survive.* Garrard, 1966.

Acknowledgments

The editors are indebted to the staff of the LIFE Nature Library volume, *Early Man.* The staff for this edition: Ogden Tanner, editor; Eric Gluckman, designer; Marianna and Jonathan Kastner, writers; Eleanor Feltser, Susan Marcus, Paula Norworth, Theo Pascal, researchers; Grace Fitzgerald, copyreader; Gloria Cernosia, art assistant.